FACING THE CHALLENGE

The Twentieth Century Fund / Danforth Foundation

The Report of
The Twentieth Century Fund
Task Force on

SCHOOL
GOVERNANCE

With a Background Paper
by Jacqueline P. Danzberger

The Twentieth Century Fund Press/New York/1992

The Twentieth Century Fund is a research foundation under-taking timely analyses of economic, political, and social issues. Not-for-profit and non-partisan, the Fund was founded in 1919 and endowed by Edward A. Filene.

Library of Congress Cataloging-in-Publication Data

Facing the challenge: report of the Twentieth Century Fund Task Force on School Governance/The Twentieth Century Fund/ Danforth Foundation.
     p. cm.
"Background paper on School boards, a troubled American institution by Jacqueline P. Danzberger."
   Includes bibliographical references and index.
   ISBN 0–87078–337–8
   1. School boards—United States.   I. Twentieth Century Fund. Task Force on School Governance.   II. Danforth Foundation (St. Louis, Mo.)
III. Danzberger, Jacqueline P. School boards. 1992
LB2831.F33   1992
379.1'531—dc20   92-15176
                                                                CIP

Copyright © 1992 by the Twentieth Century Fund, Inc.
Manufactured in the United States of America.

FOREWORD

All too often, the intense media coverage and fierce political debate about America's economic future have focused on such indicators of economic performance as savings levels, technical and scientific research, and capital investment in business plant and equipment. But as important as these indicators are, they must not obscure a larger truth: that the real foundation of a society's wealth lies in the knowledge and ability—the educational attainment—of its people. Perhaps we take this truth for granted; or perhaps we ignore it because our understanding of educational cost-benefit analysis is so limited. After all, much of what matters in education is not quantifiable, which is exactly why continual debate and study of the subject is both inevitable and important.

The education of our children is our largest collective undertaking as a society. Even now, when the nation's willingness to make commitments to public activity seems remarkably fragile, elementary and secondary schooling remains primarily a mission for the public sector. The economic arguments for this approach are in fact overwhelming. For despite the claims of a few ideologues, the benefits to society of educating each generation far outweigh the individual investments that parents, left only to their own resources, could make. It is not only right; it is in our interest to use tax dollars to educate our children. And as long as we tax to support education, we shall have a lively political debate about how to go about the task.

America has chosen to govern its vast system of elementary and secondary education through a uniquely decentralized structure. More than fifteen thousand school boards are charged with responsibility for making the decisions that govern the education of millions of children in public schools across the country.

Though these school boards must operate within a detailed web of state law and regulation, they retain substantial autonomy. An overwhelming majority of them are popularly elected. While voter turnout for these elections normally is small (in some cases negligible), elected school boards remain an expression of our belief in the desirability of the local control of schools.

School boards have become the subject of increasingly heated debate—in some cases, of criticism that goes so far as to call for their abolition. Since schools are the place where a great investment in human capital is made, these complaints may simply be a reflection of the way the nation is struggling to achieve a better return on its investment. Indeed, many citizens are demanding better results in the face of persistent challenges at home and abroad.

These developments are not really surprising. They probably should be seen as part of the larger wave of reaction to disappointing test scores, slow progress by minorities, and a perceived loss of workforce competitiveness. There is, then, considerable interest in a fresh appraisal of the role and effectiveness of school boards.

In view of the ongoing public policy debate on these issues, the Trustees of the Twentieth Century Fund approved a plan to commission a Task Force on School Governance in 1989. The decision to look at this particular aspect of our nation's schools follows from the Fund's examination of American education in the early 1980s and is part of an ongoing program examining critical social issues in America, especially urban America.

The work of the Task Force was facilitated when, in 1991, the Fund secured the assistance of Jacqueline P. Danzberger, director of governance programs at the Institute for Educational Leadership, to write a background paper and Michael W. Kirst, professor of education at Stanford University, to provide support to the members of the Task Force. They and all the members, especially Mitchell Sviridoff, who ably served as chair, are to be congratulated for their efforts.

*   *   *

A special acknowledgment is due to the Danforth Foundation, without whom this report would not have been possible. We appreciate its financial support for the project, and its intellectual input throughout the process. Danforth's support and help were invaluable to the Fund and to the members of the Task Force.

Richard C. Leone, PRESIDENT
The Twentieth Century Fund
March 1992

CONTENTS

MEMBERS OF THE TASK FORCE

Mitchell Sviridoff, *chair*
Senior Fellow
New School for Social
  Research

Sharon L. Brumbaugh
Former President
Pennsylvania School Boards
  Association

Betty Castor
Commissioner
Florida Department of
  Education

Ramon C. Cortines
Superintendent
San Francisco Public Schools

William J. Grinker
Former Commissioner
Human Resources Adminis-
  tration, City of New York

Henry F. Henderson, Jr.
President
H. F. Henderson Industries

Matina S. Horner
Executive Vice President
TIAA-CREF

Harold Howe II
Senior Lecturer Emeritus
Graduate School of Education
Harvard University

William H. Kolberg
President and CEO
National Alliance of
Business

Anne C. Lewis
Education Policy Writer

Reese Lindquist
President
Seattle Education
Association

Floretta McKenzie
President
The McKenzie Group

Howard M. O'Cull
Executive Director
West Virginia School Boards
  Association

James R. Oglesby
Former President
National School Boards
  Association

Neal R. Peirce
Syndicated Columnist
Washington Post Writers
  Group

Lourdes Sheehan
Secretary for Education
United States Catholic
  Conference

REPORT OF THE TASK FORCE

Can the United States dramatically improve the quality of the education offered its children? Can America's public education system provide students with the skills they will need in a world that is ever more complex and competitive, more technology and information driven, and more politically and economically interdependent?

As the shortcomings of our public school system have become more apparent, these questions are being asked with increasing urgency by both citizen and business groups. As a result, the nation's thousands of local school boards—the traditional linchpin of American educational governance—are facing a serious crisis of legitimacy and relevance.

Modern school boards, born in the nineteenth century and reformed early in the twentieth, were founded on the belief that citizens should control the policies that determine how the children in our communities are educated. Operating in many jurisdictions with full fiscal independence—often with their own taxing powers—school boards are the major component of local school governance across the United States. In addition, they have progressively expanded their overall management role, though often in response to state legislation.

The current debate about the future of education in America, however, has focused largely on issues such as choice, school-based management, class size, teacher preparation, and student assessment—not on the governance role of school boards. The Task Force believes that while these are critical issues, reform efforts will have only limited impact until the role of governance is addressed and the question of how basic decisions are made is answered.

The various problems facing schools and school boards tend to be most acute in major urban areas, the home of those children most affected by the social and economic changes sweeping America. In suburban and rural areas, many boards continue to play their traditional policymaking role, but that may not be enough in today's society. It will not ensure the fundamental changes America's schools require. Nor is it likely to produce a meaningful commitment to three goals this Task Force considers critical for the future: that all children should meet world-class educational standards; that there be accountability for what happens in schools; and that what happens in schools be tied to other services for children.

Based upon these beliefs, the Task Force calls for fundamental changes in the structure and operation of the institutions of local educational governance. While a separate local school governance body may well be the best choice, the role and responsibilities of such a body should be thoroughly redefined.

There are those (including some members of our Task Force) who believe that the crisis in school governance in many parts of the country is so serious that school board reform and redefinition will not do the job; they believe that totally new and radically different approaches are required in those areas. Such bold experiments may be most appropriate in our large cities where school governance has dramatically shortchanged children and society alike. Experiments already have been undertaken, including devolution of most decisionmaking authority to councils elected at the local school level (the Chicago model) and contracting out operation of all or part of a school system to a third party contractor (Chelsea, Massachusetts, and some schools in Miami). In a spirit of innovative experimentation, the Task Force believes that these far-reaching governance experiments should be welcomed and their results monitored closely for the lessons (both positive and negative) that they provide (see the list of experimental models that begins on the next page).

For the most part, however, states and communities are likely to favor less far-reaching reforms to the existing school governance system. They are most likely to support changes that will spur basic improvements in school board governance while retaining the familiar form of democratically chosen citizen boards that make the ongoing, major decisions for entire school districts.

The question that then needs to be asked is, what has made many school boards an obstacle to—rather than a force for—fundamental education reform? Our answer: The tendency for most boards to micromanage, to become immersed in the day-to-day

NEW EXPERIMENTAL MODELS

Growing concern with contemporary school governance has helped to produce a variety of new approaches. Some might work well under the supervision of local boards, but others would require far-reaching authorization under state law:

▲ *Charter schools. This idea, approved experimentally by Minnesota in 1991, goes a step farther than simple parental choice of a public school. It assumes that true choice may require entirely new schools. Any qualified institution or group—a college or university, a social service organization or team of teachers—may seek to set up a charter school. But the charter application must be sponsored officially by a responsible public body (government or school board). The charter schools must be open to all; they must be tuition free, nonsectarian, nonselective, and nondiscriminatory. For each student they can attract, they should receive from government the average per pupil amount currently provided by the state and/or locality.*

▲ *Contract out school management. Local or state authorities may decide to contract out the management of individual schools, or an entire district. Boston University, for example, runs the public school system for Chelsea, Massachusetts. On Chicago's West Side, a group of over fifty corporations has run a tuition-free model elementary school since the late 1980s.*

▲ *Competitive contracting of school management. A more expansive version of the contracting model has been proposed by Philip Schlechty, president of the Center for Leadership and School Reform in Louisville, Kentucky. Under his plan, each state would set up a public education commission responsible for ensuring that the voters in every county, city, or town may choose who would provide schooling in their community. Potential providers could obtain state charters by promising to provide equal access, transportation, racial balance, performance data, and collective bargaining rights. The choice of provider would be made through local elections, for a term as long as 10 years. The local school administration could appear on the ballot as could teachers, either independently or through their union. Schlechty argues competition on this scale is vital to move bureaucracies toward change.*

- *Merging school boards with children's policy boards. A locality might decide to merge its local education board with its children's policy board to determine whether unified policy-setting could provide a superior continuum of services for children and fewer instances of children "falling between the cracks" of the different social service providers.*
- *Site-based school management. Education policy boards have the right to delegate broad policy-setting and administrative control to individual school sites. Many are already trying; site-based management is in fact a major reform effort across the United States at this moment. Among the more prominent examples are Rochester, New York; Miami, Florida; and, with full implementation of its Education Reform Act of 1990, the entire state of Kentucky.*
- *Elected local school committees. Chicago's much-publicized system of popularly elected local school committees goes a step farther. The local committee is empowered to choose principals and help guide instructional reform; some committees have in fact sought counsel from the nation's leading education experts. (Chicago retains a central school board for a number of key functions, such as collective bargaining and the collection and dissemination of data on each school's academic performance.)*
- *Merge education into general purpose government. This option would make school districts a department of city government reporting to the mayor and city council. The policy board would become a citywide citizens' education advisory committee. Its representation would be constructed from "the bottom up," with representatives elected from groups of site-based management schools.*

And, far more radical:

- *States directly run schools. Local policy boards could choose to put themselves out of business and have the state run all schools—as Hawaii does.*

While "radical" in one respect, all of these options would remain under the umbrella of public education. This sets them apart from so-called voucher plans under which public funds could also flow to schools that are either sectarian or charge tuition, or both.

administration of their districts that is properly the realm of the professional administrator.

The Task Force believes that school boards must become policy boards instead of collective management committees. This will require granting them the policymaking latitude that would allow them to function as bodies responsible for governance; they will be responsible for setting broad policy guidelines, establishing oversight procedures, defining standards of accountability, and ensuring adequate planning for future needs. While professionals would oversee the myriad details of running public schools—as they theoretically do now—they would do so within the constraints and policy parameters established by those governing local education: the education policy board.

In addition, the Task Force believes critical changes are needed:

▲ in the way school board members are selected and trained;

▲ in the relationship between school boards and other levels of government, especially with state governments and, in the case of cities, with municipal governments;

▲ in how school boards relate to other services directed to the needs of children—health care, social services, and libraries—a particular problem in urban areas.

Without these changes, school boards will not have a strong voice in the debate over the future of America's schools.

The Debate over School Boards: Part of the Problem or Part of the Solution?

School boards can provide a valuable lay perspective on public education, a structure for public accountability, and a way for parents and the community to influence the vital policy issues affecting schools. But sadly, they often do not. Indeed, three major reports issued in 1983—the president's *A Nation at Risk*, the Twentieth Century Fund's *Making the Grade*, and the Carnegie Foundation's *High School: A Report on Secondary Education*—added up to a ringing vote of no confidence in the existing structure of public education governance. The issue of governance, however, has yet to be thoroughly addressed.

Some observers of our education system cite a bill of particulars that can be read as an indictment of the current system of school governance:

▲ Many school boards, especially in large cities, have tolerated maladministration. Boston's city government became so disenchanted with the policy paralysis of its school board that Mayor Ray Flynn jettisoned the elected board and substituted one appointed by the mayor. Moreover, school systems in Jersey City and Trenton, New Jersey, and Harlan County, Kentucky, for example, have fallen into state receivership.

▲ Though still nominally nonpartisan in most states, school boards increasingly reflect the fact that many members identify the school board as a political stepping-stone and concentrate on constituent service rather than serving as disinterested citizens focusing on broad education policy.

▲ Constructive board-superintendent relationships have collapsed almost entirely in many large cities. In 1990, 20 of the 25 largest central city school superintendencies were vacant. Most big-city superintendents do not last three years on the job, and, as a result, fewer qualified candidates apply for these posts.

▲ Many boards have become bogged down in the minutiae of routine administration and spend endless time dealing with detail. The Tucson, Arizona, school board, for example, met 172 times in one year.

▲ In the eyes of many, boards are viewed as barriers to school-based management and decentralization—a major reform movement of recent times.

▲ School board election turnouts have fallen so low in many localities—in New York City they have been as low as 7 percent (below even the dismal rates in many other local elections)—that questions have arisen about their legitimacy. In fact, practices in place in some areas actively discourage voting.

▲ Boards often fail to coordinate their activities with the general purpose institutions of local government, such as departments of health, child care agencies, and protective and juvenile services. As a result, there is both overlap and neglect in the provision of social services to children.

▲ State governments tended to bypass school boards almost entirely in the "reform" efforts of the 1980s on the grounds that school boards were not sufficiently vigilant in addressing what was taught, how it should have been taught, who should have taught it, and how results should have been measured.

There are those who, however, offer a staunch defense of the current governance structure:

▲ School boards provide local control and an accessible level of government. In a country committed to representative democracy, they provide citizen access that remote state and federal capitals cannot duplicate.

▲ School boards are thus a cornerstone of local democracy. Education is one of the ways in which youth are socialized, and communities look to their schools to impart community values to their children.

▲ Many serious governance problems—except for the prevalent state regulations that undercut school boards—are centered in large urban school districts. The large districts encompass some 40 percent of school children but only a small fraction of the more than fifteen thousand local school boards.

▲ Schools, particularly those in inner cities, are being asked to deal with increasing numbers of children with emotional, physical, and financial problems falling outside the traditional support systems that schools have established for children. Neither the schools nor the boards governing them can be held responsible for the increasingly serious problems faced by many of today's youth.

▲ School boards vary immensely in governing effectiveness and the leadership qualifications of their members. But among the thousands scattered across the United States, it is easy to find boards that demonstrate exceptional leadership and exemplary operational practices.

▲ Many of the present governance problems cannot be blamed on local school boards. State governments must take substantial responsibility for the manner in which boards function because they created the voluminous laws and regulations for which boards are ultimately responsible and which force them to micromanage. For example, the standards for student promotion are the legitimate concern and responsibility of local school boards: nevertheless, some states have imposed detailed regulations in this area.

Today's system of governance is one that largely has allowed school administrators rather than board members to "control" policy, particularly because many administrators have made it a practice to overwhelm boards with detail—and reams of meaningless paper and statistics not vital to governance. (Some colleges and universities reinforce this approach through administrator training programs.)

In reflecting on the merits of these various arguments, the members of the Task Force concluded that school boards have all too often been part of the problem. We also concluded that they can be part of the solution.

Creation of Local Education Policy Boards

Our principal recommendations originate from the conviction that solutions to the current governance problems lie in fundamentally redefining the role of school boards. As in the early twentieth century, when the restructuring of school boards embodied a recognition of the changing needs of America's children, so today fundamental reform is necessary. *School boards must assume the policymaking authority that would justify their becoming local education policy boards.*

The New Look in School Boards. The ideal local education policy board would differ from current school boards in a number of basic ways:

Policy boards would be responsible for developing strategic plans with both long- and short-term goals, objectives, performance indicators, and pupil assessment systems. As part of their strategic planning, policy boards would help define and then approve curriculum frameworks. The result would be clear and coherent policies concerning what children should know and the skills they should possess. Policy boards would not be involved in curriculum development, but would instead establish overall curriculum objectives and directions.

Education policy boards would continue to exercise overall responsibility for the budget, collective bargaining, and education initiatives. However, their performance of these functions would change significantly. They would not review all contracts that are competitively bid nor vote on contracts for limited amounts (of course, the definition of "limited" would depend on the size and budget of the district). They would establish overall goals for labor agreements and approve the final contracts, but they would not be involved in the negotiating process.

When it comes to budget and spending priorities, local policy boards would establish policies for contracting and purchasing, and hire independent auditors to review the execution of these policies. But policy boards would not supervise these arrangements to the extent that many boards now do; for example, while policy boards would continue to approve construction projects, they would not approve the purchase of pencils. For large projects, we recommend that school boards consider a "community building committee," including some board members as well as individuals from outside appointed by the board. The building committee would approve change orders and oversee construction, leaving more board time for the primary tasks of establishing, monitoring, and overseeing education policy.

Local policy boards would also ensure the creation of effective staff development policies aimed at improving many aspects of teaching. Many existing staff development programs are inadequate, often lacking the duration, follow-up, and support necessary for teachers to implement innovative and effective teaching strategies and models. This does not imply that staff development plans would be identical at each site nor that the board would manage those programs; instead, the policy board would be responsible for their creation and oversight.

We cannot stress too often that the role of these policy boards would be to establish policy and provide policy oversight, not to implement policy in detail. That is why the board would be responsible for hiring a district chief executive officer (superintendent) to serve as the administrator of the district, presiding over the day-to-day operation of the school system. The policy board would not be involved in the hiring of employees beyond a few senior administrators. Boards would not interview or approve prospective principals. Instead, principals would be selected in accordance with the personnel policies set by the board. Boards would, however, be notified of all appointments; they might also conduct periodic reviews to ascertain whether board personnel policies are being followed.

The State Role. School boards exist because state governments choose to create them. Under the U.S. Constitution, education is a reserved power of the states, but all states except Hawaii have chosen to delegate substantial policymaking and operational decisions to local school boards. At the same time, states have passed numerous regulations aimed at controlling various aspects of educational administration, ranging from requiring local boards to approve student field trips (West Virginia) to involvement in the adoption of textbooks (Texas, North Carolina, California).

One key to the success of the policy board concept is a changed relationship between school boards and state governments. Right now, the system of accountability and responsibility makes little sense. Consequently, we recommend that states repeal all current laws and regulations specifying the duties, functions, selection, and role of school boards.

Accordingly, we recommend that school boards be given the policymaking authority that would justify their being called "Local Education Policy Boards." At the same time, states should set clear performance criteria that would enable them to hold local policy boards accountable for student progress and management effectiveness.

Accountability. We recommend that third parties assist policy boards to design and implement a board performance evaluation focused on educational policy and a reallocation of board priorities away from routine administration. The accountability procedures put in place should include an evaluation of how board policies are implemented.

In addition, boards must rethink their current criteria and processes for selecting and evaluating superintendents. We recommend a stronger role for superintendents, especially with respect to their relationship with and accountability to a board that would establish broad policy frameworks.

Policy boards should use their mandate to develop strategies for improving school operations by convening community forums on major educational policy issues. Policy boards should also have the authority to appoint citizen/consultant panels to review particular issues within the school system, providing boards with the expert advice that they need to render sound decisions on issues outside their primary areas of expertise.

Today, state law requires and citizens view boards as the ultimate level of appeal for their concerns about schools, including the location of bus stops and street crossing guards. This kind of detailed supervision is exactly the opposite of what we believe school boards should be doing. Instead, we would suggest that local education policy boards consider the use of ombudsmen or administrative hearings as a recourse for citizen complaints and appeals. The amount of time boards spend handling matters such as bus routes (which often have underlying policy implications such as fairness and equity) could be reduced dramatically through the use of ombudsmen. This would allow boards to focus on the larger issues on the educational agenda and would provide them with the ability to intervene.

Local boards should also be freed of their quasi-judicial responsibilities. They should *not* preside over student or employee grievances, except in such unusual cases as the termination of tenured teachers. States could free boards of these responsibilities by chartering local mediation and arbitration panels to resolve complaints and disputes. Local jurisdictions would appoint members to such panels.

The Problem Is Not Just Education: Policymaking for Children's Services

In order to better integrate children's services, states should establish new Children and Youth Coordinating Boards.* Local education policy boards should explicitly link their education policies to broader children's issues under the supervision of these coordinating boards. Rather than take over the functions of an education policy board, these coordinating boards could have a variety of structures, varying from state to state, that would focus on the integration of children's services with the goal of preventing serious problems.

These coordinating boards would place services in the broader context in which children live—family, school, neighborhood. These boards should link and coordinate the delivery of services for children with multiple needs. The contemporary societal problems—

---

*An interesting example of this approach is the Minneapolis (Minnesota) Youth Coordinating Board (MYCB), a creation of municipal government and the mayor. Established through a joint powers agreement between the city of Minneapolis, the Minneapolis public schools, Hennepin County, the Minneapolis Park and Recreation Board, and the Minneapolis Public Library Board, the eleven-member MYCB defines its goals as promoting the integration and quality of services for all of the community's young people, not only those with special needs.

Local and state funds were made available for the planning and operation of the MYCB. Each of the five sponsoring government bodies contractually agreed to provide at least $150,000 per year for five years to support basic staffing and operating costs. The apparent success of MYCB thus far seems to be a result of the mayor's vigorous commitment to an integrated youth policy. The mayor's effort to mobilize broad community support for MYCB is invaluable in helping the board to develop neighborhood centers for integrated children's services. Indeed, schools themselves could and should become neighborhood centers available to children, parents, and the community for the provision of a range of services.

such as drugs and homelessness—facing our youth all too often adversely affect their ability to take advantage of existing educational opportunities. For example, many children experiencing difficulty in school also have health and family problems. Under the current system, children receive a label depending on where they enter the fragmented social service delivery system. They are classified, for example, as truants, drug abusers, or homeless. But the interconnected nature of their needs is often missed and their other problems overlooked.

The Role of the States

We earlier recommended that "states repeal all current laws and regulations" impeding the policymaking authority needed for local education policy boards to be truly responsible and accountable for the governance of education in their communities. *The first step in doing this is for states to review their existing statutes and regulations, many of which unnecessarily restrict the discretion of local school boards on policy matters.* For example, the California Education Code, at five volumes, is cluttered with outmoded regulations and duties required of school boards, deflecting them from their policymaking role and needlessly inhibiting local flexibility.

The problem is that state governments have gradually expanded their control over local schools in terms of both programs and personnel. Most states have assumed responsibility for making a number of important decisions affecting local school districts. State legislatures often delegate to state boards of education the power to set standards for pupil promotion and graduation. Many state boards have the authority to adopt standard courses of study and prepare curriculum guidelines in subjects such as civics and math. State boards also regulate specific instructional materials, particularly as noted, the adoption of textbooks for statewide use in all public schools.

States also have assumed authority over hiring practices through their requirements governing teacher certification. Most states now specify the minimum length of training programs, stipulate program content, and accredit training institutions.

This expansion of the state role in local education governance has resulted in rising tensions between state government and local school boards, leading to philosophical and political clashes between states and school districts. The states' constitutional authority over education is in constant conflict with the ethos of local education governance, particularly in this era of school reform activism. *The members of this Task Force believe that state governments must redress this growing imbalance in the relationship between state oversight of and local control over public education.*

State governments can assist local school boards by developing statewide indicators to measure and compare the progress achieved by districts and individual schools. These measures would help establish accountability in terms of pupil accomplishment, condition of physical plants, and, in pursuit of the earlier-mentioned goal of combining all services for children, the condition of children from birth to age eighteen. States should include recommendations for how districts can supplement these statewide measurements with indicators designed to illuminate local situations.

Financing is another difficult issue affected by the tension between state and local responsibility. States provide the largest portion of local school funds and have assumed greater authority over what may be considered local board decisions. (While the level of support varies from state to state, the nationwide average is: states, 50 percent of funding; localities, 44 percent; the federal government, 6 percent.) Moreover, state funding is uncertain, which is a serious impediment to improving local school board policymaking. For example, many states do not confirm their levels of local school aid until late summer—making long-term planning virtually impossible.

The Task Force believes that states should limit their governance role in order to foster the development of effective policy boards. To prevent poor management and policymaking practices, states should:

▲ set the broad educational goals that they believe students must achieve, without restricting the ability of local policy boards to innovate, experiment, and find ways to meet the special needs of their students.

▲ hold local school boards accountable for meeting overall ethical, supervisory, and performance standards, and have in place a set of intervention strategies to ensure that these overall standards are met (including as a first step support and assistance, with takeover as a final recourse). To aid the boards to do this, states must establish strict regulations concerning potential conflicts of interest for school board members; create specific resources, procedures, and programs to help prepare new school board members for their policymaking roles; and mandate and fund board self-assessment and development activities focused on board performance and accountability in making policy.

▲ select and support "masters"—outside facilitators with expertise and experience in education policy and school governance—to assist in local problem solving and conflict resolution. (Under these circumstances, either the school board would request a master or, based on performance indicators, the state would recommend that a local board bring in a master. The key idea is that a master would intervene before the local board's policymaking process has broken down completely, forcing the state to place the district in receivership, as has occurred in New Jersey, Kentucky, and California.)

▲ establish and make available panels of experts to work with school boards requiring assistance in areas such as strategic planning, development of curricular frameworks, review of school site performance, and staff development.

Selection of School Board Members

There is no single mechanism for selecting school board members due to the diversity of the more than 15,000 American school districts. The most common system, the local school board election, is increasingly criticized for producing unrepresentative boards as voter indifference has dramatically reduced citizen participation. ***The Task Force recommends that state and local governments take actions aimed at increasing voter turnout for school board elections.*** Furthermore, to ensure that school boards represent the entire community, we suggest that no school board election be certified by the state if less than 20 percent of registered voters turn out. If this bare minimum requirement were not satisfied, the board seats would be declared open, and the district would call a new election. In the interim, temporary appointments would be made to fill the open seats.

To encourage larger voter turnouts, school board elections (now typically held separately from general elections) should be held in conjunction with general elections. The old system was justified as a means of insulating school governance from the partisanship of national, state, and local politics, but, unfortunately, this independence is pointless when citizens neglect their responsibility.

Another obstacle to school board service is the increasingly stringent financial disclosure requirements imposed on those who would serve; these requirements tend to restrict the pool of board candidates. Disclosure is essential but should not be so intrusive that it discourages citizens from serving.

Yet another issue is pay. ***We believe that policy board members' costs, such as child care, transportation, and lost pay for time off from work (to a fixed maximum), should be reimbursed.*** Some districts have traditionally paid board members for attendance, which may be appropriate but should not be based on the number of meetings held; such a system might encourage board members to meet too frequently and to seek ways of expanding their functions into areas better left to educators and administrators. (An annual honorarium that is adjusted to reflect poor attendance may be one way to provide some compensation.)

A Special Case: Our Nation's Large Cities

The Task Force believes that additional changes are required in the governance of schools in our nation's large cities:

The Task Force recognizes the enormous variation in the way America's cities collaborate with and govern the school systems within their jurisdiction. Where city and school district boundaries are identical or nearly congruent, the Task Force supports a much closer relationship than is now common between school boards and city government in order to ensure the coordination of youth services. Focusing accountability for the coordination of education and other children's services in the office of the mayor will diminish both the overlap of services and the danger of neglect.

The Task Force also believes that in large cities the best method for choosing education policy board members would be through appointments—rather than elections—with the authority to appoint the majority of board members residing in the mayor. We further believe that these appointments should be based on the recommendations of a broadly based screening panel. (These panels should represent the widest possible range of policy and racial/ethnic perspectives, and they should include people from all income levels.) This would encourage greater collaboration between schools and city government, meeting our concern that children receive the necessary full range of social services.

Collaboration between local school boards and city governments would also deal with an important fiscal reality—that most major city school districts are dependent on local government for support. Having a direct relationship with city hall might create a better climate for budget negotiations and financial support for education. Now, all too often, the needs of our cities' children are sacrificed to the limited political agendas of those who may be using their office as a stepping-stone to a political career or to promote special interest agendas that have almost nothing to do with education.

While we believe appointing a majority of school board members in cities is the right approach, we recognize that this reform is not likely to come about right away. In the short term, we recommend fundamental changes in the way school board members are elected. A key difference between the way America's large cities and smaller communities govern their school systems is the election process for board members. In most communities, board members are selected through at-large elections, but many cities elect board members by geographic precincts, which often results in members viewing themselves as representing only their own district's interests. In such cases, board members often promote their individual district agendas at the expense of broader policy objectives and long-term planning.

At the same time, geographic selection provides minorities with the opportunity to serve on school boards as well as giving stronger representation to the range of viewpoints that at-large elections tend to obscure. ***Therefore, we recommend a mixed system of at-large and district-based elections, when elections are required, with the expectation that a majority of a local policy board would be made up of those representing a citywide perspective.***

Conclusion

If America is to continue to play a role as a world leader in any arena—business, politics, security—it must suceed in reforming its public education system. Reform of any kind requires political will, and that, in turn, requires vision. If the experiences of the last few years have taught us little else, they have taught us that the rest of the world is not standing still. The time has come for our leaders to take responsibility in this critical area. More than ever, our national leadership must support the concept of a strong public education system, and our state leaders must initiate and carry through a thorough reform of the existing system of school governance.

The distinctive hallmark of American education for more than one hundred and fifty years has been the local school board. It served us well in creating a literate, innovative society that has changed the world. We do not think anything would be gained by shifting to a totally new system. Enduring institutions are the heart of a strong democratic society. However, we believe fundamental changes are necessary in the way schools are governed. Indeed, we believe that school boards are no longer providing the quality leadership needed to secure America's future. *Our recommendations are aimed at transforming one of America's great institutional innovations, local school boards, into a force for reform, creativity, and support for the real needs of children. Without the kinds of changes we recommend, the whole debate over education will be hollow, filled with wonderful concepts and ideas and without a structure that can make reform a reality.*

SCHOOL BOARDS:
A TROUBLED AMERICAN
INSTITUTION

Background Paper by
Jacqueline P. Danzberger

It must be remembered that there is nothing more difficult to plan, more doubtful of success, nor more dangerous to manage, than the creation of a new system. For the initiator has the enmity of all who would profit by the preservation of the institutions and merely lukewarm defenders in those who would gain by the new one.

– Machiavelli

Acknowledgments

Many individuals provided assistance and support for this paper. I especially thank Michael Usdan, president of the Institute for Educational Leadership (IEL), and Michael Kirst, professor of education, Stanford University. They generously permitted me to borrow from the book we are writing on school boards and provided helpful reviews of this paper.

I am also grateful for the assistance of Michele Clark, my colleague at IEL, who conducted the search of the literature and provided particular help on the history of school boards.

Steven Greenfield of the editorial staff at The Twentieth Century Fund provided very helpful assistance in the evaluation of the paper.

And, finally, I thank Liz Corn and David Corn for their dedicated work in the production tasks for this paper. I thank them also for their patience in seeing the project through to the end.

Jacqueline Pilcher Danzberger
May 1991

INTRODUCTION

Local school boards are one of the United States' most vener-able public institutions, embodying many of the nation's most cherished political and cultural tenets. One of these tenets is a distrust of "distant" government that dates back to colonial times, when Americans were governed, often unjustly, from afar. Lay school boards are also valued because of the traditional American ambivalence regarding experts and their expertise. This profound ambivalence accounts for much of the fervor for elect-ing laypersons to serve on school boards, which are then expect-ed to act as buffers between citizens and possible "excesses" of professional educators. Historical experience also explains Americans' fondness for independent school boards. In the late nineteenth century, city school boards controlled by the politi-cal ward system were enormously corrupt; this led to drastic changes in education governance. The present-day commitment in the vast majority of school districts to separating education governance from municipal government—to keep education out of the hands of "ordinary" politicians—is rooted in these century-old reforms.

The structure of local education governance is simultaneous-ly sustained by and broken down by our inability to reconcile deeply held beliefs with current realities. This is particularly true in the major urban school districts. It is time for enlightened and dispassionate dialogue about the governance of public educa-tion. Such dialogue will require suspending presuppositions about the "one best system" and forgoing unjustified blanket indictments of local school boards.

The issue for debate is not local control (as many defenders of the status quo would have us believe) but how to achieve and assure effective local governance of public education. Citizens can continue to exercise control over the education of their children while also having effective leadership and management of education through strengthened, reformed, or changed governance. Indeed, such effectiveness will be essential if we are to have any hope of systematically reforming the educational system and of setting much higher standards of educational attainment for all students.

The governance structure has basically served this country well since the first school boards were established in Massachusetts more than two hundred years ago. Serious questions about local education governance are, nevertheless, hardly new. In the late nineteenth century, education governance in the cities was in chaos. Although the reforms enacted brought some order, they also brought bureaucracies that gradually eroded community representativeness. In the counterreforms of the 1960s and 1970s, school boards were made more accessible and representative. Over time, however, this counterreform movement has also contributed to the governance problems and highly politicized school boards evident today in major urban school districts.

Problems in local governance are not limited to the cities. The essentially rural, small-town state of Kentucky recently enacted legislation to restructure its education governance system.

In some school districts, school boards provide outstanding leadership. Satisfaction with school board leadership is most prevalent in communities with homogeneous populations, few financing problems, and a consensus about educational goals and values. In addition, school board service in such districts is infrequently used as a stepping-stone to higher political office. These districts are, in the main, those of the nation's more affluent suburbs.

Questions about, and outright attacks on, school boards have reached a point where, if for no other reason than prevention of further erosion in the public's confidence in boards, we need to pay serious attention to how public education is governed. The Twentieth Century Fund and the Danforth Foundation established a Task Force on School Governance in 1990 for the purpose of providing the first national forum to examine the institution of school boards and discuss thoughtfully the many governance alternatives and reforms that are surfacing at the behest of national education reformers and state and local politicians.

The Rationale for a Dialogue

The national education reform agenda has changed. It has moved from doing "more of the same" within the existing structure to strategies for basic restructuring of the schools and to expanding educational decisionmaking for and about schools to hitherto excluded groups—teachers, parents, and community members. This second wave of reform is already forcing de facto changes in traditional roles and the authority of boards. The question is not whether there will be change, but whether or not local governance will be reformed in the context of the current governance structure and as a result of thoughtful deliberations.

Although governance is but one variable in the education reform equation, how school boards govern affects all the other variables. School boards are counted on to provide leadership for public education that mirrors the needs of students and the values of the community without surpassing the fiscal resources of the taxpayers. In theory, boards reconcile these three basic considerations through well-informed dialogue and then adopt appropriate policies. Boards are also expected to carry out five essential management functions of leadership: (1) planning and priority setting; (2) organizing and institution building; (3) keeping the system functioning; (4) agenda setting and decisionmaking; and (5) exercising political judgment.[1]

School boards are responsible for a major task of leadership—explaining to and teaching the community not only about education issues and the educational needs of students but also about the district's goals and strategies.[2] We look to school boards to envision goals and to plan for the future, to motivate staff and students through policies that set high expectations, and to support the work of staff and students in achieving these expectations. Boards are expected to serve as a symbol within their communities for the importance of education and its place above the fray of petty politics and self-interest. School boards are also expected to achieve a workable consensus among their members, to help in resolving conflicts within the school system, and to be sensitive to the need for organizational renewal and change. In addition, school boards are now called on to provide what John Gardner defines as "boundary crossing" leadership—connecting with other agencies, organizations, and institutions whose policies and practices affect children and adolescents, and their families.

Given the performance expectations for school board governance, to measure current realities against aspirations amounts to "looking through a glass darkly," particularly in the major urban school districts. But the same dark vision might well apply to the performance of the U.S. Congress, certain state legislatures, city councils, county boards of supervisors and mayors, and, in the opinion of many, the White House Domestic Policy Council. There is no obvious movement documented on the op-ed pages of newspapers, in current books, or issuing from national task forces to debate continuation or radical restructuring of the nation's federal, state, or local governing institutions—except for school boards. It is beyond the scope of this paper to provide an explanation for why we, as a people, accept less than effective leadership or failure in these other governing institutions with much greater equanimity than we do in education governance. However, it is possible to suggest some informed theory for this singular position school boards occupy.

Americans truly believe that education can make a difference in their lives, and their childrens', even when an individual's personal experience with formal education may have failed her or him. In school, children are inculcated with the founding fathers' belief that a people free but ignorant will not long remain free; they carry that tenet into adulthood. We have looked to our public schools to make us a nation, and there is no other institution that touches us all in the same way. We also generally accept that a strong and globally competitive America rests on an improved educational system.

It is probably safe to say that the calls by our political leaders at all levels of government and within the business community for radical educational reform are not driven by a concern for the inner life of children and adults. These influentials increasingly question whether school boards can provide the requisite leadership to change the system to respond to the nation's economic challenges, or whether they are actually impeding systemic education reforms.

School boards themselves will benefit from a national dialogue about school governance. Described as "that dark island of American governance," school boards, says Neal Peirce, are "the institution that everyone knows of but few understand."[3] Moreover, although the concept of school boards is strongly supported among citizens, very few bother to vote in school board elections, and fewer and fewer wish to serve on them. Grass roots apathy or complacency about school boards may very well be explained by lack of public understanding of the policymaking process and the way elected board members deal with constituent concerns. Any governing institution little understood by those on whose behalf it governs will slowly atrophy absent rigorous examination. Without direct and systematic confrontation of the issue of school governance, there will be a succession of "guerrilla" attacks on or piecemeal changes in the roles and authority of school boards that will occur without the benefit of dialogue to define expectations of school governance. These expectations need to be clarified and the current system measured against the expectations. We need, in short, a dialogue that produces thoughtful, well-founded, and defensible rationales for continuing, modifying, or structurally changing current education governance and its functions. Without such a dialogue, we shall find ourselves going down a road without knowing where we are going, or if we arrive at the desired destination.

About This Paper

This background paper was written for the Twentieth Century Fund-Danforth Foundation Task Force on School Governance in order to provide a common base of information about American governance of public elementary and secondary schools, the major problems school boards encounter in trying to provide effective leadership, and to suggest various possibilities for strengthening or restructuring local education governance. The paper, along with the recommendations from the deliberations of the Task Force, is also intended to stimulate and help inform dialogues about education governance in states and localities across the nation.

The paper argues for putting governance on the national education reform agenda, either to strengthen the current system or institute moderate to radical changes. The range of ideas presented illustrates the variety of directions that changes in governance might take. In order to be consistent with the broader purposes of this background paper, no specific suggestion is endorsed. Rather, states are urged to encourage and support broad discussion and local experiments to strengthen, reform, or restructure governance of the public schools. There may be no one best way to govern public education, but to ignore the very real problems of local school boards would be a disservice to the mostly well motivated, hardworking, and volunteer individuals who serve on these boards and to the students and citizens on whose behalf school boards govern.

CHAPTER 1

LOCAL GOVERNANCE AND
EDUCATION REFORM

S chool boards are empowered by the states and responsible to their constituents for providing leadership and governance to achieve educational objectives for all students. Increasingly, though, politicians, business leaders, experts in education governance and, indeed, the mass media and the public are questioning whether local school boards as currently structured can provide the forward-looking leadership and effective governance required by an increasingly complex education reform agenda.

THE NATIONAL EDUCATION REFORM AGENDA

Throughout the 1980s, experts and citizens alike sought the cause of the malaise in public K-12 education, looking first at one element of the institution of schooling and then at another. In the first wave of reform, the answer appeared to be "more." State legislatures, assuming a much more assertive role in local school districts, required more math, more science, more tests (for students and teachers), more English, and so forth. The spate of state-legislated reforms largely excluded local school boards and superintendents from the dialogue and political processes. Attention soon turned to those who teach. The question became how to turn what had become a trade into a profession. Interestingly, even though hundreds of state task forces and "blue ribbon" committees sprang up, they largely ignored the plight of at-risk students. The first reform wave appeared oblivious to demographic reports documenting that children from historically at-risk families and minority racial and ethnic groups were growing as a percentage of the youth population, and that children were becoming the nation's poorest citizens.

The second wave of the education reform movement has been marked by a much broader appreciation for the complexity of the challenges, both from a standpoint of teaching and of governance, involved in improving the educational attainments of America's young people, and has focused particular attention on urban school districts. There is general agreement that the issue of learning goes far beyond "how much." It concerns instead at what level learning takes place and how it should be structured. Efforts to improve teaching are now concentrating on how teachers are prepared and then sustained in their professional development, not just on matters of pay levels and incentives. Until the last three or four years, no politician would have supported the establishment of an explicit set of national education goals, let alone a national assessment of education. The doctrine of local control, or as some might say, the myth, was believed sacrosanct. Now, members of Congress and state legislatures, governors, and others in the political realm have endorsed national goals for education and openly discuss national testing or a set of national expectations for student learning.

In this current wave of reform, the issue of local governance has moved into the spotlight. Boards and superintendents were rarely involved in the policy process that produced the first reforms, largely because of the perception that leadership of local school districts—particularly the school boards—were part of the problem. The school board community responded by raising the flag of "local control." But in no state did boards or superintendents, acting collectively through their state associations, put forth a reform agenda, produce a cogent analysis of the issues, or seriously question the structure, processes, and content of public education.

This is not to deny that school boards initiated reforms or provided leadership for the improvement of schooling. The Institute for Educational Leadership (IEL), in its 1986 study of school boards, documented the success of a number of school boards in instituting many early reforms, such as student testing, graduation requirements, and curricular reforms.[1] In fact, in districts with acceptable student achievement or better, the establishment of minimum state standards had a negative impact. For example, state-required norm-referenced testing (which simply assesses students against a national sample of their peers) imposed a backward step on districts that had moved to criterion-referenced testing (which provides an analysis of achievement against expectations based on student ability that can guide curriculum and teaching). Mandating paper and pencil tests in order for children to move from kindergarten to first grade hindered districts that were attempting to move to a much more flexible developmental educational philosophy in the first two years of formal schooling.

However, nationwide, school boards were not in the lead in bringing concerns about the decline of public education or the proper role of governance to the attention of the populace. Nor were those involved with the education reform movement ready to take on the issue of governance at first. As a result, the early reforms simply ran "end plays" around the role of the boards by legislating in areas hitherto held sacrosanct by local decision-makers: testing, curriculum content, teacher qualifications, minimum achievement levels for every grade.

Reformers have been peeling away the layers of the schools' problems now for several years, slowly realizing that the reforms have wrought few improvements and that our schools require basic restructuring—from how learning is structured in the classroom to who makes decisions about schooling. Finally, more and more influential reformers, including the intellectual engines of reform—business leaders, political leaders, and, increasingly in the cities, coalitions of citizens from all sectors—have begun to realize that local governance of schools must undergo serious scrutiny.

Mayor Flynn of Boston has abolished (with state concurrence) the elected Boston School Committee and created an appointed school board responsible to the mayor and the city council. In Chicago, a broad coalition of business leaders, political leaders, parents, and concerned citizens forced the state legislature to place individual school governance in the hands of the schools themselves. Several states, heeding the call of a 1986 report of the National Governors' Association, have passed legislation that allows them to take over and direct operation of school districts that continue to fail to educate students. The New Jersey State Department of Education exercised its right to take over the

Jersey City public schools. The state of Missouri attempted (but failed in the courts) to place the Kansas City public schools in state receivership, citing the school board's seeming inability to govern the district in a fiscally responsible manner. In one city (Chelsea, Massachusetts), the school board itself handed the nuts and bolts of governance and management over to Boston University, reserving to itself oversight of the contract with the university. The Kentucky state legislature, faced with misconduct by district leaders and the abysmal performance of school districts in the eastern counties, and following a decision by the state supreme court that the system for school financing was unconstitutional, started tabula rasa, restructuring the entire state system for public education, excluding nothing from possible elimination or radical change. In the final legislation, Kentucky kept the local school board structure but instituted sufficient controls to preclude any reversion to business-as-usual by school boards.

Local school boards have moved front and center in the education reform debates for many reasons. Undoubtedly, the appalling state of public education in the cities has been a major reason. Indeed, governance is now perceived as one of the greatest barriers, if not the primary obstacle, to systemic reform of education. A corollary phenomenon is the apparent inability of urban boards and their superintendents to develop working relationships. The 1990-91 school year saw an unprecedented number of urban districts with superintendent vacancies. The Council of the Great City Schools, a membership organization of the nation's largest urban school districts, reports that the average tenure of superintendents in these school districts is now less than three years. The implications of this turnover for education reform are devastating. Since it is the board of education that hires and fires superintendents, eyes have naturally turned to the role of the boards in the hiring process and to their ability to develop productive relationships with their chosen executives. But there is another aspect of this issue: the urban superintendency is itself fraught with problems.[2] Serious shortcomings in superintendents' preparation and administrative experience contribute to the rapid turnover. This issue is discussed in greater detail in chapter 3.

It is now almost axiomatic that improved schooling depends on better health and living standards among the children and adolescents served by the urban districts. Creating a tapestry out of the loose threads of services used by these children and their families requires real collaboration between governmental structures that have been deliberately isolated from each other since the early twentieth-century governance reforms. This is a major ambition of the second wave of education reform. All the available information suggests a lack of communication and coordination among the providers of human services. Interviews with mayors and city council members in the urban case study districts for IEL's 1986 study made clear that the separation of education from other governing responsibilities was not causing "sleepless nights" for these politicians, who were generally grateful that they could be removed from the problems of the schools and the issues that create highly charged emotional climates for political decisionmaking by school boards.[3]

Efforts to create collaborative solutions and new structures for service delivery to meet the needs of urban children and their families are under way in many communities. Some leadership among national organizations is beginning to emerge, as evidenced by the development of a draft national policy at the February 1991 Wingspread conference jointly sponsored by the National School Boards Association and the National League of Cities. School boards have long said that they could not "do it alone" and that there was a limit to how many of the noneducational needs of children schools could meet under their traditional structure and financing. However, until very recently, neither the school boards nor general government took the lead in attempting to reorganize and consolidate childrens' services, redefining lines of authority and use of resources. Bringing the agencies of government together will be a daunting task.

Student and parental choice about the schools students attend is currently a burning issue with clear implications for governance. The philosophical underpinnings of the debate over choice reveal a tension between two fundamental American values—the separation of church and state and the inherent validity of marketplace forces. For professional educators and to some extent the public, choice is an American heresy because it requires turning away from a historic article of faith about "one best system" of education as described by David Tyack.[4] Others, among them John Chubb and Terry Moe in *Politics, Markets and America's Schools,* call for total dismantlement and the creation of a system that would allow schools to be established privately and licensed directly by states, with schools responsible to the state much as school districts are now.[5] The system proposed by Chubb and Moe would not preclude the continuation of school districts and school boards, but the schools they would run would be but one option available to students and families. Public school districts would have no greater call on the resources of the state than would independent schools within a state's "public" system of choice.

Critics of the proposal advanced by Chubb and Moe (and of other "choice systems" involving private sectarian and nonsectarian schools within the current governance structure) raise questions about the ability of families to make informed choices and caution that the loss of the common public school may compromise the nation's ability to educate a citizenry with any shared sense of national history or values. Critics also point to the danger of fragmented community institutions, which might further pull apart community social structures.

The major reform strategy now being tried by many school boards is the granting of greater autonomy to individual schools. This strategy responds to a set of studies known as the "effective schools" research, which makes a compelling argument for educational decisions being made as close to the point of interaction between teacher and learner as possible. Devolution of decisionmaking authority is congruent with the move to "professionalize" teaching through the granting of greater freedom to control one's own professional practice and more formal recognition for particular expertise.

Moving the governance of schools to the school site frequently involves parents in policy advisory groups or in actual decisionmaking, determining goals and objectives and use of resources for individual schools. The Chicago governance reforms, which established local school-site councils, are a radical example of this devolution of authority. Many urban districts are initiating site-based management as the keystone of their restructuring efforts. Notable examples include Rochester, New York; Dade County, Florida; and Los Angeles and San Diego, California. No school district has enough experience with site-based management to document either improved student performance or widespread renewal of professional morale and leadership. The Chicago reforms, although admittedly just a year old, have shown relatively little teacher involvement in school dialogue and decisionmaking, with few exceptions apart from those teachers elected to the local school councils.[6] A suburban district near

Washington, D.C., instituted a pilot project in school-based management, but one school withdrew after a year, citing teacher complaints that the responsibilities were excessive, although they did concede that the experiment had been interesting.

Experience to date with the movement to school-based management illustrates the peril inherent in the more widely touted reform strategies—advocates tend to oversell their cause, and school officials and representatives then rush to "get on board" before finding out if the train can reach its destination. It makes a great deal of sense for schools to be more responsive to the particular needs of their students. It also makes sense to allow those working with the students to make decisions about how educational objectives might best be attained. As with many reforms (whether these deal with curricula or decisionmaking), however, they will likely be carried out by administrators and teachers whose training and experience ill equip them for many of the new roles and expectations demanded of them. Particularly in the large and bureaucratized urban districts, the professional behaviors now desired by reformers—initiative, dialogue about substance and methods of teaching, in-place leadership, and so forth—have been previously discouraged and are seen, in too many school districts, as unwelcome and unsuitable.

Leaders from all quarters of society, even the White House, are calling for systemic changes in public education. Nonetheless, organizational change is beyond most educational administrators' training and experience, and is equally beyond the governance capabilities of most school boards. Further, sweeping reorganization will produce high levels of political and institutional discomfort. School boards that are committed to systemic change need strong and continuing political support from reform advocates at the national and state levels, and from their communities.

SCHOOL BOARDS AND EDUCATION REFORM

School boards and their statewide associations have serious concerns and frustrations with having been shut out or "end played" by the states in the shaping of education legislation and regulatory actions during the great waves of reform from 1983 to 1990. IEL found in its 1986 study that this frustration stemmed not so much from power politics as from a genuine concern about the nature of the state reforms, and states' development and monitoring of regulations without the experience of those governing and administering the schools. Board members also pointed out the loss to states that did not seek advice from school districts whose own experiments, in many instances, had far outpaced the legislated reforms. The IEL study confirmed that most boards in a sample of nine metropolitan areas had already instituted many of the components of their states' reforms prior to the states' initiatives.

In a large suburban district in Texas (basically composed of mid-level, white-collar professionals and the working class), board members and district administrators were supportive of state education reforms because they recognized that there had to be dramatic steps to improve education in the majority of Texas school districts. However, they believed that some of the reform legislation was so misguided educationally that it was bound to cause enormous problems. They believed the prior involvement of board members and professional educators could have helped the state reforms. The suburban school district leadership proved its prescience: the paper-and-pencil test mandated by the state for promotion from kindergarten, cited as the prime example of educational folly, has been abolished by Texas.

An analysis of local governance performance and education reform must recognize two distinct waves of state reform since 1983 and consider the performance of local governance against their very different characteristics. It is also important to keep in mind that states' original reform initiatives were driven as much, if not more, by external pressures (national reports, the business community, and special interests) than by gubernatorially or legislatively initiated concerns about education.

School Board Reaction to the First Reform Wave

The major challenge to local governance in the early stage of reform was the increased prescriptiveness of the states in areas such as curriculum, teacher tests, student tests, graduation requirements, and so forth. The Center for Policy Research in Education (CPRE), which prepared a study of state education reforms,[7] documented two findings from this first period that are most pertinent to an assessment of school boards and education reform. First, the states tended to avoid enacting measures that were complicated or difficult to implement. The other discovery was that there was very little resistance from school boards to reforms that involved increased academic content or requirements. In fact, there was evidence of districts using state reform policies to promote local priorities. School boards, contrary to what their most avid critics write, may try to provide leadership to improve local education or meet the needs of unserved student populations but find that local political support does not exist for such initiatives. A state mandate removes the political problem and allows a board to do what it knows must be done. A case in point from the 1970s is the embracing of special education legislation by the majority of school boards. Without state and federal laws, the majority of boards would not have been able to dedicate local resources to a small student population needing extra attention to the full extent the law required.

The positive track record of local boards in implementing and even exceeding state reforms does not appear to have resulted in increased confidence in local boards' ability to initiate and govern educational change.[8] And boards' strong performance with state reforms through 1988 has certainly not quieted the critics. In fact, local and national media attention to school boards has risen to new heights very quickly. The explanation for this lies, in large part, in the shift in the reform agenda over the past two years.

School Boards in the Second Wave

The leadership of boards is critical to the success of reforms such as those of the second wave that require basic organizational change, devolution of or at least broadened participation in education decisions, a shift to greater accountability for student achievement, further rigor in the curriculum, linkages to agencies providing other essential human services, methods of easing the transition into the world of work, and greater equity in access to quality education. Systemic change is painful. People or institutions legally endowed with power do not readily give this up. Chubb and Moe argue strenuously that this consideration by itself makes the case for breaking up the current system in which school boards govern a public monopoly endorsed by the states.[9] Still, those with power prefer survival with diminished power to outright extinction. Therefore, it is difficult to predict how resistant school boards will be to top-down reorganization in the face of calls for national standards and curricula, as well as the appearance of legislated choice in over a dozen states.

Can local school boards as currently constituted provide the leadership for systemic change? The data are not encouraging.

Boards themselves are doubtful: school board self-assessment data from the IEL 1987-90 "Study of School Board Effectiveness" confirm that boards view themselves as less than effective in areas critical to the demands for improved leadership for and results from education reform.[10] Participating boards rated themselves particularly low on meeting regularly with local government officials or other bodies to discuss education and related issues. The self-assessment system, instrument rating scale, and national sample are described in the notes to this chapter.[11] Boards recognize that they need leadership training as well as dialogue with the community to define areas of governance responsibility if they are better to meet constituents' expectations.

THE IMPACT OF EDUCATION REFORM ON LOCAL GOVERNANCE

The education reform movement has considerably strengthened the power of the states in relation to the historic discretionary power of local school boards. However, the local governance structure remains unchanged. No state other than Kentucky has initiated discussion of the basic roles and responsibilities of local governance.

Two national studies of urban school districts that enacted major reforms incorporating greater school-site autonomy have found no evidence that these initiatives caused the school boards in these cities to analyze the governance structure.[12] New policies to implement greater decisionmaking at the school site do not explicitly define roles and obligations of the school board vis-a-vis schools. Schools are discovering the boundaries of their "autonomy" case by case. In one large city, the central board has retained the right to veto any specific portion of a school's plan, even if it has been approved by both the school site council and a districtwide review council. The Rand Corporation's study, *Educational Progress: Cities Mobilize to Improve Their Schools*, found that the school boards in six cities subordinated their traditional roles to the community effort for systemwide improvement. However, these behaviors are not generally embedded in district policies and are therefore vulnerable to political changes and turnover among board members and in the superintendency.

State policymakers implied their lack of confidence in school boards and local professional leaders by excluding them from shaping education reforms in the 1980s. Many state policymakers also openly expressed their belief that local education leadership had failed and that states had to take the initiative and become much more prescriptive and intrusive in local education policy. Yet state policymakers not only avoided discussion about possible changes in the governance structure, but took no initiatives to strengthen the current system of local governance. A few states have mandated individual training for board members, but this is very minimal (two sessions or a few hours) and is largely informational. The challenges local boards face in responding to mandated reforms, the national reform agenda, and increasingly overt criticism have awakened state school boards associations to the recognition that their constituents are in trouble. Many of these associations have instituted programs of workshops to "certify" board members. While these efforts are laudable, the programs have not generally made use of external analysis of governance issues, and they continue to focus on individual members, not school boards as corporate governing bodies. It is in the exercise of collective governance that many boards fail.

CHAPTER 2

EDUCATION GOVERNANCE IN
THE UNITED STATES

A national dialogue about education governance requires basic understanding of the governing system and its history. This chapter describes the governance structure for public elementary and secondary education in the United States, the historical development of local school boards, and the state-local governance relationship.

THE ORIGINS AND DEVELOPMENT
OF LOCAL SCHOOL BOARDS

The early New England colonists were, in considerable number, a literate people. Their Calvinist religious heritage, which placed a high premium on personal knowledge of the Bible, greatly influenced the development of a mandate for compulsory education in America. In 1642, Massachusetts passed the first law requiring parents to send their children, and masters their apprentices, to school. With subsequent modifications, this model established in colonial New England became the basis of public education throughout the colonies and, eventually, the new republic. Each town was required to provide for the schooling of its children. Control of the school was vested in the selectmen, a group of men responsible for administration of all aspects of the life of the community, and each man became responsible

41

for a specific administrative task, such as choosing the teacher or curriculum.

As populations grew and school enrollment accelerated, so did the burdens of administration. The selectmen began to appoint a special committee in each town for the express purpose of governing the schools. This committee, the prototype for today's local boards of education, gradually assumed legal authority. Since that time school boards have constantly redefined their policy and administrative prerogatives as local, state, and eventually the federal government became involved to differing degrees in the affairs of the schools.

As populations grew, so did the physical perimeters of communities. Individuals left the towns proper to settle and establish farms in the outlying areas, rendering impractical the notion of a single school in the middle of the town. Because the farmers were taxed to support the town schools they did not use, they prevailed on the town proper to refund the appropriate proportion of tax used to finance the school and applied this money to their own rural schools. Thus, the idea of separate school districts was born. In 1891 in Massachusetts, this de facto arrangement was confirmed by state statute, which vested responsibility for its schools in each community. Each school district was given the right to set its own budget, select the teacher, determine the curriculum, and provide general oversight. Unfortunately, the seeds of still-vexing problems with local control were also planted. States required each district to accept fiscal as well as administrative responsibility for the education of its students. This policy created (or had the potential to create) inequalities among districts. Some districts were extremely poor and had few well-educated citizens; consequently, their schools were meagerly funded and poorly managed, and the quality of instruction was poor. The better-off citizens in such districts simply sent their children to private schools (in the English tradition), and public education was reserved for the poor and the disenfranchised.

The first comprehensive plan for a state school system, presented to the Virginia Assembly in 1779 by Thomas Jefferson, was entitled "A Bill for the More General Diffusion of Knowledge."[1] Although his bill did not pass for some time, this piece of legislation paved the way for Virginia, and later other states, to provide for a statewide system of not only primary but also secondary schools, paid for, in part, out of the state treasury. As the country grew and new states took shape in the wilderness, their constitutions acknowledged the need for an educated citizenry. States made provisions to establish, supervise, and finance schools within their own territories. The importance of education in the fledgling nation can be seen in the Ordinance of 1787, which set up the machinery for organizing the Northwest Territory (comprising present-day Ohio, Indiana, Illinois, Michigan, Wisconsin, and part of Minnesota). The territories had to dedicate a fixed portion of each tract of the then federal land to a school. Local control continued to reinforce the principle that each community or district could establish for itself the schools that it felt appropriate. The more affluent citizens in New England and the South continued to send their children to private schools.

It was not until 1837, however, when the first state board of education was established, again, in Massachusetts, at the urging of Horace Mann, a member of the state legislature, that states began to assume legal administrative responsibilities for the education of children. The Massachusetts state board, and those modeled after it, was originally chartered to assist local communities in providing improved education for their children. In his position as the first secretary of the board, Mann sought to "inform and unify the public" on issues of education.[2] His most notable contribution was to gain public respect and support for the state board of education and the state superintendency. He was the first to develop active state involvement in education; in 1852, Massachusetts passed this nation's first compulsory school attendance law. By 1860, most states had established guidelines for different administrative functions, school financing (in large part through the management of federal land-grant funds), programs of instruction, and teacher selection. During the nineteenth century, public education received more state funds than any other public service sector.

Despite acquiescence in a strengthened state role, a certain degree of public suspicion was still to be reckoned with, taking the form of frequently complex layers of legislation carefully setting forth the administrative prerogatives of state and local officials. State departments of education were kept small and largely clerical in function. Local control was preeminent, and school boards represented the members of each local community. As cities became the hub for newly arrived immigrants, factory workers, and industry magnates, urban school districts served an increasingly complex and diverse population. School board members were tied to municipal political structures through election by wards. This method ensured broad political representation but brought along in its wake the spoils from political patronage. School boards were frequently at the center of volatile partisan politics in the latter part of the nineteenth century.

SCHOOL BOARDS IN THE TWENTIETH CENTURY

The beginning of the twentieth century marked a shift in school board control. In 1893, there were more than 603 school board members in the 28 cities with populations of 100,000 or more, or an average of 21.5 board members per city. By 1923, this average was reduced to 7.[3] The decrease resulted from a carefully orchestrated shift from multiple boards or committees in cities chosen via partisan elections to small, central school boards selected through districtwide, nonpartisan elections. This shift in governance structure was in fact the primary objective of sweeping educational reform at the turn of the century.

During the period between 1890 and the early 1920s, the nation underwent rapid population growth fueled by a massive influx of immigrants, many of whom were from cultures and societies very different from the dominant, native-born population. Concentrated urban growth and a burgeoning industry (along with the birth of a new class of social leaders, the industrial magnates) that brought the United States to a position of world prominence drastically reconfigured the economic, social, and intellectual landscape of the country. These developments were quick to influence the course of school governance.

Across the country, groups of intellectuals, drawn from the newly emerging business and professional classes, began to lay the foundations for their own interpretation of education reform. Joel Spring writes that

when the elite business and professional groups began to dominate and control school boards, they did so in the name of "public interest." They claimed to know what was in the best interest of the educational system and the education of the child. Their claims to knowledge of the public interest in education were based on the assumption that those who had the most education in society were successful in life and had the most knowledge about educational needs and goals.[4]

A fundamental change in the decisionmaking structure was the primary objective of the reformers. To do this, they first set about to replace the decisionmakers. Under the ward system, school board members had been elected by constituencies in individual city wards. Hoping to gain control of the schools and bring order, the new elite sought to insulate education from the vagaries of political influence and partisanship. For the leaders of the movement, the rationale was simple. "One cannot expect the reform of urban education from those who serve as board members. It will have to come from the leaders of the intellectual life of the city."[5]

To the public, however, the arguments were couched in slightly different language. The reformers argued that school board members elected by individual wards tended to represent parochial interests at the expense of those shared by the entire community. According to the logic of the reformers, at-large elections would guarantee the election of board members who had the needs of the entire district at heart.

Reformers in Cincinnati were successful in having state law changed so that school board size in urban areas in Ohio was reduced from 30–40 to 7. Election by district (ward) was subsequently made citywide. Candidates were elected to the school board from among a slate carefully screened and backed by the Citizens School Committee. "The School Board as a representative form of government came to mean representation of the views and values of the financial, business, and professional communities."[6]

The industrial elites and their cousins in the professions established this new governance system in concert with the major education reformers in the early days of the twentieth century. In this restructured system, the leadership role of the school district superintendent paralleled the leadership role of corporate executives, and their relationships to their boards were essentially the same. Increasingly, board administrative subcommittees—along with their decisionmaking capabilities—were reduced, if not totally eliminated. The agenda and other initiatives were turned over to the superintendent.

Members of these "reformed" school boards were frequently heads of major businesses and therefore constrained in their ability to participate actively in school policy debate. They began to depend increasingly on the superintendent, placing their faith in the new and popular theory of scientific management. The selection of the superintendent became a critical function of the local board of education. As university presidents, the social peers of the industrialists, allied themselves with the reform movement, school administration began to receive specialized attention among education professors, giving birth to administration as a "learned profession." The school board essentially served as a buffer between the public and the professional administrators and provided the official "seal of approval" for the actions of the professionals.

Centralization of school board elections made it difficult for average citizens to seek board election because they lacked power bases, access to the media (newspapers), and sufficient financial backing. The new, small central boards and districtwide elections produced little diversity among school board members. A typical sop to diversity is illustrated by the unspoken policy of the Cincinnati Citizens School Committee. Those in control of the committee allowed a token Catholic (but from the "right" sector of society) on the board in recognition of the city's large Catholic population.[7]

Following the governance reforms and the professionalization of educational administration, school boards became more detached from the day-to-day responsibilities of running schools and from what was going on, particularly in the urban districts. Detachment from the "pulse of the people" eventually led to troubles for the "reformed" school board.

Counterreforms: Sputnik and the Civil Rights Movement

The 1950s and 1960s marked the beginning of a serious reevaluation of the nation's education system and a renewed grass roots interest in the running of the schools. During the late 1950s, attention focused on curricular rather than administrative changes, as the Soviet launch of the Sputnik satellite in advance of our own space efforts caused a crisis of confidence in the adequacy of teaching, particularly in the sciences. Governance structures of schools remained unchanged until the civil rights movement gave strident expression to the voices of minorities and the politically disenfranchised in the 1960s. Increasingly, urban schools were attacked for having failed their students and for being unrepresentative of the school district population in their governance and staffing. Parents started to complain that the education system was not sensitive to their needs and that they had no connection with district decisionmaking.

The question of broad-based school board representation has been asked and answered differently by each successive group of education reformers. Each cycle of reform has decided that the preexisting structure was ineffective and has called for a new system of representation. Invariably, this resulted in a change in the election process of the boards. Since the middle of this century, debate and subsequent changes in governance have concentrated on whether schools are best governed by a broad representation of the entire community—regardless of the members' educational, professional, social, or economic backgrounds—or by a group of individuals coming from the well-educated and "successful" population groups.

Observers and critics of school boards today vary in their analysis and in their conclusions. Conversations among prominent "board watchers" reveal little agreement about alternatives for change or root causes of governance problems as distinct from general societal problems. The one consensus reached is that local governance is not working well in too many school districts. The Institute for Educational Leadership's 1986 study of school boards produced findings and conclusions that support current observations about school boards. Among the study findings:[8]

1. There is strong support for maintaining the basic institutional role of the school board as interpreter of the community and protector against the excesses of professional educators.

2. Board members are increasingly perceived as representing special interests, and the trusteeship notion of service in which board members represent the entire community is no longer dominant.

3. Boards, particularly in urban areas, have become more representative of the diversity in their communities and often include leaders from disparate constituencies within the larger community.

4. Local boards and their members have only sporadic interaction with general government and tend to be isolated from mainstream political structures.

5. Board members are seriously concerned about the growing intrusiveness of the states as the reform movement evolves.

6. Board members continue to grapple with tensions over the gray areas between a board's policymaking and the superintendent's administrative responsibilities.

7. The need for school board individual and team training is recognized generally, but too often training is merely informational and episodic.

8. Urban, suburban, rural, and small-town boards alike find more commonalities than differences among the challenges to their effectiveness. These include public apathy, lack of public understanding of the role of boards, poor relationships with state policymakers, a lack of strategies to evaluate board performance and an intrinsic inability to focus on education issues such as improving teaching in the framework of collective bargaining.

The most severe critics of local governance, among them Chester Finn, call for the elimination of school boards altogether. "Does this legacy of our agrarian past," asks Finn, "make sense for our high-tech future?"[9] Citing the increased participation of the states in school finance and structural reform of education, as well as the growing popularity of parental and student choice and the concomitant shift in emphasis toward the individual school instead of the district, Finn concludes that local control should be reinterpreted to mean building control. The "middle manager" position of the school district board—between the states and local schools and parents—will not be necessary, he argues, as site-based management gains credibility and assumes larger proportions.[10]

Others believe that the role of the local board in educational governance should be strengthened. The greatest debate is in fact occurring among those who accept this opinion. However, in spite of strong support at the local level for school boards, there has been no real attempt to mount a counterforce to the growth of states' authority nor even to respond to school board critics. School boards and the school board community (their state and national associations) could take the initiative to examine local governance—in fact, it would be to their benefit to do so. But self-examination in any institution is rare. With a guaranteed clientele and governance of a monopoly, school boards do not possess the incentives to initiate basic system reforms that would produce high levels of institutional discomfort.[11] The response to problems tends to be, "Our school system is fine. The problems are somewhere else." And, according to most published national polls, the public also believes the problems are in other districts, not in theirs.

School boards' own perception of their leadership role has not been clearly defined. A Rand Corporation recent study investigated six major urban districts that had succeeded in improving their local schools. The researchers found that "school boards seldom invented or motivated the school improvement efforts. . . . In most cities, the board has been a player in someone else's leadership strategy."[12] According to the Rand study, the one exception is in San Diego, where "the board, in the process of searching for a new superintendent, initiated a comprehensive review of goals and priorities which eventually became the mandate for the new superintendent."[13] The study confirms the importance placed on selection of the superintendent. It is less clear that boards have a commensurate commitment to forging a good working relationship with the superintendent they have chosen.

The Politicization of School Boards

Ironically, the highly politicized school boards of today (most significantly in the urban school districts) grew out of the reforms of the 1960s, which were implemented to counteract the undesirable side effects of the depoliticizing governance reforms instituted at the turn of the century. As we have seen, the near-sacred belief that education should be divorced from politics is rooted in late-nineteenth-century municipal corruption. Ward politics controlled who taught, who was awarded contracts, what textbooks were purchased. Urban schools were governed by a ward-based, decentralized committee system that reached the pinnacle of absurdity in Philadelphia, which had 559 school board members serving on 43 elected district school boards in 1905.[14] Cities did not have school systems; they had political fiefdoms.

Urban systems had become as unmanageable as they were corrupt. The need to reform governance fit in well with the growing fascination with rational management theories. Ellwood P. Cubberly, one of the leading education reformers, thought that businessmen would make the best school board members. They were, he said, "used to handling business rapidly, were usually wide awake, and were in the habit of depending on experts for advice."[15] The reformed structure of municipal education governance complemented the rise of the professional superintendency in the latter part of the nineteenth century. This shift in the control of schools away from the grass roots toward small boards dominated by business leaders and the professions endured in the cities until the 1960s. Even today, outside the cities, most school board members are from business or the professions, or occupy the same socioeconomic strata. Surveys of school board members reveal that the overwhelming majority are college-educated, male (approximately 33 percent are female), white, 45–60 years old, and have family incomes in excess of $50,000.[16] Contemporary similarities with those who served on school boards during the heyday of the "trusteeship" notion do not necessarily mean that boards continue to govern with that same notion away from the cities—indeed, many boards do not.

Analysts such as Michael Kirst at Stanford University point to the late 1950s as the watershed period when the public confidence in school administrators and school boards began to fade.[17] The *Brown v. Board of Education* Supreme Court decision called attention to the abysmal education afforded black children in the South's segregated systems, and alarm about Russian scientific and technological superiority at the height of the cold war caused fear across all sectors of American society. During the 1960s, minority enrollments increased in major urban school districts. Whites began their exodus from the cities and the schools; eventually the movement metamorphosed into a flight by the middle and upper-middle classes that cut across racial lines. The civil rights movement led to scrutiny of our public institutions and doubts about the ability of affluent whites on school boards to represent the needs and concerns of minorities in the cities.

In response to the ferment, New York City was divided into community school districts charged with governing all but the secondary schools and districtwide programs such as special education and vocational education. Many cities moved in the 1970s and 1980s from school boards elected citywide to discrete electoral districts. Some instituted a combination election that continued to elect a minority of members citywide. Concurrently with these counterreforms, special interest constituencies grew in all districts as the schools added more and more categorical programs through federal and state legislation, for example, special education, gifted and talented education, Chapter I (originally Title I), bilingual education, and so forth. The United States began to spend much more on public education, giving rise to watchdog groups monitoring the distribution of dollars. Demands for responsiveness and participation grew across the nation in all types of communities. School district administrations and school boards scrambled to establish community advisory groups to work with districts on everything from curriculum to communications. Neither the district bureaucracy nor school boards relinquished authority. They did, however, become much more embroiled in constituent politics. In the cities, the politics began to turn the school boards into the most contentious of public institutions. Meanwhile, more and more children were failing in the urban school districts. The counterreforms succeeded in returning authority for the schools in the cities to those whom the schools served, but the responsiveness of school district bureaucracies changed little. This can be attributed in part to the nature of bureaucracies, but it must also be laid at the door of the highly politicized school boards, unable to pursue coherent and continuous policy initiatives.

THE GOVERNANCE STRUCTURE

The governance of public elementary and secondary education reflects two cherished American beliefs—first, public education must be governed by lay authorities, and, second, governance must be decentralized to assure local control. The U.S. Constitution does not mention education; therefore, the provision for and control of education is a power reserved to the states, as expressed in state constitutions. Although these constitutions vary, all of them (with the exception of Hawaii; and Hawaii is now proposing decentralization of its state system) have delegated authority for the governance and operation of schools to local school boards. The organization of school districts varies from state to state (and even within states), but the governance structure does not.

The States
The states' two-tiered governmental framework lodges responsibility for public education with the states but leaves operation

of the schools to local school districts. Some states operate schools, but these offer specialized instruction—regional vocational schools, special schools for the arts or for math and science, and so forth. States govern through state boards of education and administer education through their departments of education, typically headed by a chief state school officer (commissioner or superintendent of education) appointed by the state board. In a few states (for example, California, Arizona, and Indiana), education commissioners are chosen via statewide election. Most state boards are appointed by the governor. In states with elected chief state school officers, one can often find a commissioner hailing from one political party while the appointed state board owes its loyalties to another. Some states, notably Illinois and Kentucky, that traditionally elected their commissioners of education have changed to appointed commissioners. Indiana attempted a similar reform, but powerful political forces (unlikely bedfellows, the Indiana Education Association and county political party chairs) prevented it.

State boards of education have historically played a fairly passive role in shaping public education, the notable exceptions being the New York Board of Regents and the California State Board of Education. Until the 1970s, state departments of education were relatively small organizations. They certified teachers, collected data from local districts as required by state and federal law, and "policed," although not aggressively, local compliance with state laws and regulations. Until a sharp increase in state funding that accompanied the reforms in the 1980s, state financial support for local school districts averaged around 35 to 40 percent of local budgets.

The states' influence began to increase dramatically in tandem with the increased federal role in education following passage of the Elementary and Secondary Education Act in the Johnson administration, desegregation of many urban school districts mandated by federal courts, and legislation such as the Education for All Handicapped Act, directed toward guaranteeing rights protected under the Constitution. In effect, the states were made responsible for implementation and monitoring of the federal legislation. Federal legislation also recognized the limited capacity of state departments of education and provided funding for their development. The federal categorical programs also provided funding for staff and other administrative costs attendant to the administration of federal education programs. To this

day, approximately 50 percent of the cost of staffing state departments of education is supported through federal dollars.

The states' prominence in public elementary and secondary
educational governance vastly increased with the state legislative reforms of the mid-to-late 1980s and a more aggressive leadership among a "new generation" of chief state school officers.
Local school boards across the land feel the "heavy hand" of the
state in areas hitherto sacrosanct to local determination—a new
prescriptiveness in curriculum matters, mandatory statewide
testing of students (in some cases requiring the use of state-
developed tests), testing of entry-level teachers already certified
by a teacher preparatory institution, increased student graduation requirements, and so forth. The increased role of the states
brought more regulations to assure local compliance and,
inevitably, increased reporting and paperwork. But the expansion of states' roles and mandates also brought new state funding into local districts.

The separation of the governance function at the state level,
as carried out by state boards, from other government functions
mirrors the pattern at the local school district level. The effectiveness of this separation is being questioned by at least one
state leader, Governor Weld of Massachusetts, who has proposed
abolishing the state board of education and moving to a system
in which the commissioner of education would be appointed by
the governor and become a member of the cabinet.

Other changes in the wind for state governance are arising
from the redefinition of the roles and responsibilities of state
boards and education departments away from a focus on
enforcement of standards and monitoring of local districts toward
providing resources, expertise, and technical support for local
reform efforts.

Local School Districts

In the United States, more than 15,000 local school districts
are responsible for over 90,000 schools; 80 percent of these
school districts have fewer than 3,000 students. A few states
have separate elementary and high school districts; some states
have mainly county districts with independent city districts; and
still others have township, city, and consolidated districts. In
some states, notably in New England, most school districts correspond to the jurisdictions of towns and cities. School districts
are as diverse as the populations they serve,[18] ranging in size

from the massive districts of New York or Los Angeles to sparsely populated rural districts that share their superintendents with adjacent districts, to nonoperating districts existing merely as legal and fiscal entities.

As populations moved westward after the Revolutionary War to settle the interior of the country, new outlying districts gradually formed and were given the legal authority to control their own schools. But these small, newly autonomous districts created consternation among educators. Horace Mann, one of the preeminent nineteenth-century educators, was a leading critic of this trend in education governance and strongly questioned the ability and willingness of these school districts to provide adequate schooling.[19] Despite Mann's misgivings, this system of smaller geographic school districts spread throughout the country, except in the South, where the county became the basic unit of school governance. Countywide school governance continues in the South and some border states. The county governance structure helped protect against the highly politicized, ward-based school governance in northern cities in the late nineteenth century.

State legislatures have been reluctant to meddle in traditional structures of school district organization. When municipal districts were consolidated from wards into citywide bodies in the early twentieth century, the initiative came not from state legislators and policymakers but from a coalition of reform activists. Consolidation efforts spread successfully outward from the cities, with a wave of nonurban mergers occurring immediately after World War II. In 1920, there were 130,000 school districts in this country. By the early 1980s, this number had dropped to slightly more than 15,000. Consolidation has not been uniform across the country: five states—California, Texas, Illinois, Nebraska, and New York—contain nearly one-third of all the nation's school districts. Although debate about consolidation continues to rage, few studies have attempted to measure the optimal size of a school district because no one can agree about the importance of the relevant criteria. Arguments about the economics favoring large districts serving more students are offset by the realities of the high cost of transportation and auxiliary services required by such complex and massive organizational structures. Attempts to consolidate small districts in rural communities are stymied by a fierce allegiance to home rule, the strong community identification with the local high school, and resistance to perceived interference by "outsiders."

Types of School Districts

While the consolidation of school districts has redistributed students and shaken up communities throughout the country, the basic structures of the districts themselves have remained untouched. Each state classifies its own school districts, which are generally organized along one of the following three lines:

Unified School Districts. These districts provide K–12 instruction for all public school students. Some unified districts include junior college programs as well. Whether the district is comprised of a one-room schoolhouse, as in some rural areas, or more than one hundred schools, as in large urban centers, it is all under the authority of one school board. The American Association of School Administrators' (AASA) Commission on School District Reorganization concluded that "the unified, or 12-grade, school district which is adequate in size has proven to be the best system of school government devised by the American people."[20]

Separate Elementary and High School Districts. Elementary school districts operate K–6 or K–8 schools that feed into geographically larger secondary school districts. In 1977, 608 districts—most of them in California, Illinois, and Montana—were offering only secondary education. Many observers believe these districts, which are located for the most part in large metropolitan areas, provide some of the best secondary education in the country. However, schools in some of these districts have fewer than one hundred students and offer sorely inadequate programs.

Specialized Schools. Many states have established regional secondary schools for vocational education. Local school districts provide funds to help pay for the cost of educating their students in these schools. A few states operate statewide schools, usually for the arts but more recently for science and technology. (North Carolina, for example, has established statewide residential high schools.) Local districts sometimes agree to act regionally to provide special programs like nonmainstream special education.

Except in New England and most cities, school districts are not generally defined along town/municipal boundaries. Although bound by the laws of the municipality, local school districts are autonomous and, in the main, fiscally independent taxing authorities. City and county districts, by way of contrast, tend to be fiscally dependent, relying on city councils or county boards to approve budgets and levy taxes. In Connecticut, all school districts are fiscally dependent. Ninety-two percent of all school districts in the United States are fiscally independent. Yet the issue of fiscal autonomy is being fiercely debated. Supporters of autonomy believe it is critical to keep school government distinct from general government to prevent a recurrence of the political corruption of the nineteenth century. Critics contend that fiscal control should rest with the municipality, and that fiscal independence has led to waste and inefficiency with inadequate public accountability from school boards.

Governance of Local School Districts

In every state except Hawaii, local school districts are governed by boards of education that are separated from general government. Although deriving their authority from the states, the local school board members are still subject, in most states, to individual recall elections just like other local officeholders. A notable exception is Connecticut. That state's constitution is so explicit about the state's responsibility for education that the Connecticut state supreme court ruled in the late 1960s that because board of education members are legal agents of the state they may not be locally recalled.

Ninety-five percent of all local school boards nationwide are elected; appointed school boards occur mostly in the cities. One exception has been in Virginia, where currently all school boards are appointed; however, the governor of Virginia signed legislation in April 1992 allowing elected school boards. Most school boards are nonpartisan, and to further guarantee that school boards are protected from the political fray, elections are generally held in the spring or summer. In New England, however, board elections coincide with November general elections. Connecticut, along with most southern states, elects school boards through political parties. Most school boards have tax-levying authority, with the collection of school taxes typically carried out by the unit or units of general government. Until the great spate of state reforms in the mid-1980s, local property taxes supplied most of the funds for school districts. Now the state share of financing for local education averages more than 50 percent across the country. The ability of school boards to raise funds through additional taxes has been substantially circumscribed in several states (for example, California,

Massachusetts, and Minnesota) because of taxpayer revolts that resulted in capping local tax increases and state efforts to equalize expenditures among school districts.

School boards are charged with the responsibility for hiring a superintendent who must meet state certification requirements for the superintendency. The superintendent is both the school board's chief executive officer and the professional leader of the school system. Individual members of school boards have no authority. Authority lies only in the action of the board as a whole. The role of the contemporary school board is the product of over two centuries of evolution, but has changed little in the past eighty years. The local school board is the only means through which the community expresses directly its opinion on education affairs. School boards, acting on behalf of their fellow citizens, are supposed to interpret the community's educational needs and demands and translate them into policy. They are also required to mediate conflicting interests, sort out contending educational values, provide leadership, and initiate and enact local policies to respond to state and federal statutes that specify responsibilities and determine the limits of school boards' discretion.[21]

The role of the board in any school district is defined in large measure by state constitutional and statutory provisions that frame the mandatory and discretionary aspects of school boards' responsibilities. Court decisions, attorney generals' opinions, and rules and regulations of state boards of education further circumscribe the work of boards. Expectations of individual board members, current and past relationships with teachers and other employee groups, traditions of the district and the culture of a local board, and the strength and style of a superintendent affect a board's role. The media affects the work of school boards and citizen opinion. Voter behavior and the educational expectations of interested citizens and parents affect both a board's definition of its role and its governing behavior. School boards frequently govern in ways that reflect the social and political attributes of their school districts: divided communities tend to have conflicted school boards. School boards are the crucible wherein the community's deeply held and often conflicting opinions about education are supposed to be forged into some consensual direction for the schools.

Elected or Appointed School Boards: Does It Make a Difference?

The late Francis Keppel, a renowned American educator, noted that:

for a number of years, researchers have examined personal characteristics of board members: education, occupation, age, income, etc., in an attempt to see which selection method—appointment or election—results in the most competent members. Insofar as personal characteristics indicate competence, the assertion that one method is superior to the other has not been supported by research. In fact, comparison of elected and appointed board members reveals more similarities than differences.[22]

Students of local educational governance continue to search for the one true method of school board selection, but, as Keppel suggests, it is probably a futile search.

In districts with elected boards, the voters directly choose those whom they want to govern the schools. This meets a basic purpose of local governance of the schools: a school board that reflects community values and expectations. On the downside, however, voters tend to perpetuate the status quo and to expect schools to replicate the kind of education they experienced when they were in school. This is particularly characteristic of rural and nonmetropolitan small-town school districts.

In the past two decades, elected school boards in the cities have become much more representative of urban diversity. Individual board members, even where all are elected at large, tend to have different constituencies or are elected on the basis of narrow issues. Although these boards are representative, the members represent conflicting issues and goals among the citizens. Governance catatonia frequently results. The problem is exacerbated in school districts that elect individual board members from discrete electoral districts. The Institute for Educational Leadership's 1986 study of school boards clearly revealed that board members elected in this manner are subjected to much greater constituent pressure and, consequently, voted much more frequently according to constituent demands than did members on the same board who were elected at large.[23] The "trusteeship" notion of board service, with its focus on the district as a whole, was totally foreign to these board members.

Based on these observations, one might assume that a board appointed by a mayor or a county council or board of supervisors would behave less divisively and therefore provide more effective governance. But the example of Jersey City, New Jersey, says otherwise. Before the state took over the Jersey City school district, the school board was appointed by the mayor, who by all accounts appointed a board representative of the political dealmaking and patronage excesses of city hall. For a more "genteel" example of political influence, turn to a suburban school district in northern Virginia, where members of the county board of supervisors appoint the school board. When asked to whom they are primarily accountable, most members of this board of education replied, "to the supervisor who appointed me." The circumstances are further complicated in that county government is elected by party, adding another layer of political allegiance. The politicization of the board is especially evident in the rocky board-superintendent relationship. However, in a neighboring, and far more heterogeneous, Virginia county, the school board is appointed in exactly the same manner but is rarely contentious and is perceived as providing fairly good leadership and governance for a much more challenging school district. Here, the board and superintendent are considered an effective team.

If the existing board selection process is seen as deficient in any school district, it should be changed. If a state or school district determines, for example, that the only way to make school boards more accountable is by linking them to the political accountability of general government, then appointed boards will meet that specific objective. But changing over to an appointed board will not necessarily achieve widespread education reform objectives. New York City's central school board is an appointed body, and public education in that city is in wretched condition. Chicago, excoriated in the 1980s by William Bennett, then U.S. secretary of education, as having the "worst schools in the nation," had a school board appointed by the mayor.

If the broadest possible political representation is desired, then election of board members by discrete electoral districts will achieve that objective. If the goal is effective, consensual leadership for a troubled district, then districtwide elections for all board members would appear to be in order. If the objective is forward-looking school boards (in contrast to those intent on maintaining the status quo), the challenge is then to raise the community's expectations, not to change the way school boards are selected. In a rural school district concerned about the exodus of young people, a school board (whether appointed or elected) that initiated an educational program designed to expand students' horizons and expectations would not hold office for long.

How school boards are selected is therefore not the determining variable in governing performance, except perhaps where boards are elected from individual electoral districts. The laudable objective of making boards more representative of those using the schools in the cities may very well have contributed to the current governance chaos. How one views the results of the reform of the past two decades in many large cities depends on one's political values and priorities for what society wishes to accomplish through the public schools.

STATES AND LOCAL BOARDS

The progressive evolution of the power of the states to standardize public schooling, write Tyack and James, is a "tale of reformist battles won and further professional goals to accomplish."[24] Others, as far back as nineteenth-century state legislators setting up districts in the newly annexed western states, would choose less elegant words to describe the epic war between state and local governments for control of the schools. We speak of an American education system, but there really are fifty different systems ranging from a state with no local school boards to states with more than a thousand local school districts. It is difficult to find any state that has struck a successful balance between local and state control in the eyes of both local and state policymakers. Certain configurations have been harmonious. Local systems have frequently benefited from state intervention as, for example, when the state was given the management responsibility for federal land-grant subsidies. At other times, however, this mediating role between local and federal government has resulted in acrimony, as evidenced in harrowing cases of court-enforced desegregation requiring a call-up of the National Guard. Polarization of control usually takes place at the expense of the well-being of the educational system. Calls for state control result, in large part, from perceptions of failure, but the ensuing state-directed efforts have produced little measurable improvement in student achievement, particularly in the cities, in the years since the first wave of education reform initiatives.

The Growth of State Departments of Education
In recent years, the role of the states has received increasing attention. Increased state responsibility in funding, the call for

greater local educational accountability, and state collective bargaining laws have all projected the states into positions of
greater power and visibility. Many observers project a continued
increase of control at the state level in the future. The reasons
given are:

▲ Education is a state and not a local function.

▲ Local school districts have delegated, not plenary, power.

▲ States are increasingly interested in the operations of
schools and were the initiators of the first wave of legislated education reforms.

▲ There is an increasing demand for state money.

▲ Taking their cue from the "new federalism" of the Reagan
years, the governors played a dominant role in setting the
current national educational agenda.

Caught up in the momentum of the civil rights movement of
the 1960s, states became more involved in local school issues
as agents of desegregation and managers of federally allocated
categorical funds for students with special needs. State involvement in educational matters escalated during the 1970s in such
areas as teacher certification, school improvement efforts, minimum competency testing for students, and curriculum reform.
The school finance reform movement demonstrated that the
property tax structure was inherently unequal, and states
assumed more of the burden of financing. By the early 1980s,
state governments were, on average, providing more than half of
the current local operating funds for education. The national
mean proportion of support among the three levels of government is now 39 percent local, 56 percent state, and 5 percent
federal.

States and Curriculum Reform

Advocates of statewide education reform suggest the creation
of "a coherent system of instructional guidance, the purpose of
which is to ensure that all students have the opportunity to
acquire a core body of challenging and engaging knowledge,

skills and problem solving capabilities."[25]Obviously, a critical step is state development of a curricular framework. California is one state that has successfully developed curricular frameworks in a number of subject areas for use in the local school districts.

State-level involvement in the development of curricular frameworks, however, is not without its drawbacks. Chief among these is the tendency for curricular recommendations to be translated into demands for specific study materials. Several large states have enacted legislation requiring centralized textbook adoption, giving them undue clout over textbook development across the nation. Texas and California alone make up almost 20 percent of the U.S. textbook market,[26] leverage the textbook publishers ignore at their peril. During the 1960s and 1970s especially, the content and quality of textbooks often reflected the whims of a variety of special interests groups in California, North Carolina, and Texas, to the embarrassment of education leaders. Many critics believe that decisions about materials are best made by those closest to the students, and this view is gaining ground in state legislatures. Harriet Tyson-Bernstein writes that "legislatures have forced state agencies to yield some ground to those who believe that statewide adoption is an inherently flawed system."[27] For those states wanting to continue to develop statewide curricular frameworks, Tyson-Bernstein's injunction is to stay out of the commercial marketplace: "Adoption-state leaders should cease the practice of issuing detailed, skill-oriented bid specifications to publishers."[28]

States and Systemic Change

Students of educational reform will agree that a critical impediment to developing and sustaining change in our nation's schools is the school system itself. Over the years, different reform movements have deposited their layer of influence onto a preexisting frame, leaving an impenetrable monolith of unmanageable proportions. Much like the first archaeologists to discover Troy, education scholars are likely to descend seven layers into the depths, thinking that each layer represents the whole, until they realize that all layers are Troy.

At this juncture, therefore, it is of no benefit to assign yet one more layer to the structure. In order to break up the monolith and refashion education from top to bottom, many advocate increased state involvement. The states are not only well-positioned as potential agents of school reform (primarily through their growing share of local financial support, their capacity to monitor and upgrade teaching standards, and their intensifying role as arbitrator in issues of equity and distribution of resources), they also have a state constitutional mandate to provide adequate public education within their boundaries.

Thoughtful advocates of state reform agree that care needs to be exercised in drawing new lines for local-state relationships. The first step requires the clear "conceptualization, communication, and measurement" of education goals so that support can be mobilized at the community and state levels on behalf of the students. Once the goals have been established, the next step will be to create a "coherent system of instructional guidance" that ensures all students will receive the knowledge and develop skills and abilities necessary for obtaining employment or pursuing postsecondary educational opportunities. The glue that will hold this together is an examination of the policies and responsibilities of each level of the governance structure so that all levels operate in support of each other and of the implementation of these reforms.[29]

Concerns of Local Boards

The newfound activism of states stems from a loss of confidence in the ability of many local districts to provide high-quality education. Originally prompted by an outcry that "our schools are failing our students," states have now become concerned with economic competition. The initial phase of state involvement was comprehensive review and upgrading of instructional programs. This focus on instruction subsequently led to the development of more rigorous measures of performance for students and more stringent requirements for teachers.

The discretionary zone of local superintendents and school boards became squeezed into a progressively smaller area during the last two decades. From the top, local discretion has been pressed by the growth of the federal government, state government, and the courts. From the bottom, boards' discretion has been squeezed by such forces as the growth of local collective bargaining contracts reinforced by national teacher organizations.[30] According to Michael Kirst, this trend must be arrested and reversed. Kirst is quick to say, however, that we are not witnessing the rise of a centralized educational system. He equates the current situation, rather, to a "fragmented oligopoly" in which myriad external governing bodies and influence groups vie for a portion of local control. "So," he says, "the issue is not so much centralization in policy influence, but the progressive loss of local school board and administrative discretion."[31]

The Institute for Educational Leadership's 1986 study documents serious concerns among members of school boards about the growing intrusiveness of state legislation and regulatory authority.[32] These concerns were not simply about who is in charge, but reflected a growing uneasiness about local boards' continuing ability to respond to very real local needs. Dangers do attend the use of sweeping and aggressive state education policy. Policy changes through statute and regulation have a standardizing effect and can be absolutely counterproductive if the result discourages school responsiveness. Many states' reforms have intruded into instruction, an area of traditional local control. IEL data showed 85 percent of the boards in the sample believed their states were becoming more directive overall, and a majority believed that the state was creating more board agenda items.[33] Boards in the sample of nine metropolitan areas across nine states, and boards in three rural states, all believed their state's influence was growing, but they recognized some benefits. These boards were not crippled but did see a definite deterioration in their ability to respond to local conditions. Generalizing about the impact of diverse reforms at the school level across the states is difficult; however, the incremental growth of state involvement may prove more significant than any spurt of state legislative initiatives, such as took place in the mid-1980s.

Local boards, in general, do not understand why state authorities have lost confidence in them. Board members complain that state policymakers ignore the aggregate and cumulative effect of state policies and regulations on state-local governance patterns. As local boards see it, various crises and calls for change from powerful external forces trigger quick state responses and new mandates. These, over time, become a staggering set of rules and regulations that show little coordination and coherence and may even contain outright contradictions. School boards are also increasingly troubled by state mandates that carry no or inadequate financial support for implementation. Given the current financial straits of both states and localities, this issue is likely to erupt in conflict at some point.

Local school boards would like to become recognized and effective partners of state policymakers. But school boards have to confront the fact that the states' initiatives are, for most state policymakers, a direct response to perceptions of a lack of local reform initiatives from either school boards or professional administrators. The pattern of local school boards playing a reactive role to state policymaking continues.

CHAPTER 3

SCHOOL BOARDS:
A TROUBLED INSTITUTION

What is the condition of local education governance? Do the problems of school boards, particularly in the large cities, provide evidence that local governance is in need of strengthening, and possibly reforming or restructuring? An examination of self-assessment data from school boards and a discussion of the state of school board-superintendent relationships and the institutional problems affecting school boards can help to answer these questions.

If a school board's basic purpose is to represent the community, then there is little to debate. School boards are representative of their communities and may, far more than many "board watchers" and national "reformers" would like to think, fairly and accurately represent the values and the perspectives of their constituents. School boards in communities with highly educated citizens never make a decision that deviates from the communal expectation that children will achieve at the highest national levels and go to "good colleges." School boards in rural areas and many small towns also make decisions representative of their constituents, who place great value on tradition and who fear that greatly expanding horizons through future-oriented education would mean the loss of their young people to other places. Urban boards, too, are made up of people who, by and large, represent the diverse values and issues among their constituents.

School boards are charged with far more, however, than representing the populace. They are expected to lead and to govern the education of the young on behalf of their communities and collectively on behalf of their states and the nation. The evidence is beginning to mount, particularly in the cities, that, in this regard, school boards are an institution in trouble. Critics find evidence that local boards are increasingly irrelevant in light of the major education reforms affecting governance—the increased contribution of the states to the financing of local education, restrictions on local autonomy caused by the legislation, mandates, and increased prescriptiveness on the part of the states, the devolution of decisionmaking to the school site, and the move toward local and statewide choice in the schools students attend.

Other critics point to the drop in educational achievement generally, and especially in the urban schools, as an indictment of school board performance. Demographic changes in the student populations of cities and the older, inner ring of suburbs, say the board watchers, did not happen yesterday. Boards might have responded with a concerted analysis of these students' needs and a reform agenda long before the situation got out of hand, but there is little evidence that they did. Business leaders and business organizations have accumulated countervailing evidence from their problems in finding employees who can meet entry-level employment standards. Business also decries a dropout rate that has consistently hovered around 25 percent during the last two and half decades while increased educational achievement and higher-order skills have become critical to the nation's economy. There is also a good deal of evidence about dysfunctional conflicts on boards, again, particularly in the urban districts, gathered through media reports; in a few cases, illegal and unethical behavior has been documented.

Other evidence that the time may be ripe to look at the role and performance of local school boards comes from the 1989 Education Summit of the nation's governors and the White House, and from open discussion of ideas that would once have been considered politically untenable—a national high school examination, a national curriculum, and national achievement standards and goals. In a 1989 Gallup poll, respondents overwhelmingly (ranging from 69 percent to 77 percent) supported a national examination.[1] Parents answered even more favorably. This should not be taken at face value because the respondents were not asked questions that would tend to cast the implications of national testing in a different light. For example: "Are you willing to relinquish any say in your child's education?" Or, "Do you believe that your community has different needs and/or values from some other communities?" Nevertheless, if we assume the polls are representative, the public believes there is a national interest in public education that may have to be met in some kind of national framework.

What criteria might school boards and the public employ to assess the effectiveness of education governance in their communities? John Carver offers a cogent explication of basic principles of governance that might be used as benchmarks.[2]

1. The board is accountable to the public for the totality of the performance, destiny and behavior of the organization [school system].

2. The board, as a body, has the responsibility to serve the general public rather than subgroups of the population or the professionals whom boards employ.

3. The board exists to govern the school system not to manage it. Board members are not supposed to be administrators of the system.

4. The board has multiple and varied responsibilities (fiscal, employer, etc.), but involvement in the detail of these concerns should never displace students as the central occupation and focus of attention of the board.

5. The primary obligation of leadership is to define and attain that for which an organization exists, in this case, successful education of the students, and not to become embroiled and participants in the detail of how the ends are met.

6. The board is obligated to assess its ability and performance in governing the school system and to obtain whatever training, data and knowledge are necessary to govern effectively.

There are very few extensive studies of school boards. The Institute for Educational Leadership's 1986 study was the first since the late 1960s focusing explicitly on boards. The contemporary body of literature on school boards is mostly composed of journal articles, chapters in a few books, doctoral theses, and media articles. There are no controlled research studies that isolate variables in governance behaviors and assess impact on degrees of success in specific education reforms.

Because school boards must conduct their work in public, how they govern is a matter of public record and observation. The evidence indicates that the majority of school boards do not spend much time on board development and training, do not regularly assess their governance performance, do not have effective communication and planning with units of local general government, do not work at attaining a productive relationship with superintendents, do not provide regular community forums to educate the public about national, state, and local educational issues, and so on. If a board meets well over one hundred times in a year, insists on approving all district administrator appointments, and has agendas filled with operational/administrative items, it does not require controlled research to know that such a board is spending too little time on education policy, policy oversight, and leadership for public education, and that the board will have increasing problems in its relationship with the superintendent. If the problems of a board result in constant turnover in superintendents, systemic education reform cannot be achieved.

SCHOOL BOARD PERFORMANCE

Perhaps surprisingly to some critics, school boards know they have problems. This was documented in the 1986 IEL study and more recently in IEL's self-assessment data.[3] While there are obvious limits to the degree to which self-assessment data from a self-selected sample of boards can be applied to all boards, and limits to the usefulness of information that is inherently subjective, these results constitute the only existing national data base about school board governance, performance, and leadership. The data substantiate the major findings from the 1986 study.

Generally, school boards rated themselves least effective in the functions and behaviors for which boards are most faulted by informed "board watchers." While the boards in the sample may have been slightly more generous in their assessments of their own performance than external observers would have been, both see serious problems in the core elements of governance—leadership, planning and goal setting, involving parents and the community, influencing and relating to external agencies and organizations (such as municipal government, state policymakers, or agencies serving children, youth, and families), and policy oversight. Superintendents rated their boards as well as or somewhat more favorably than the boards rated themselves. This belies popular and media-driven perceptions of what superintendents think of boards. It is possible that the superintendents in the sample were concerned that, despite all precautions, their assessments would fall into the hands of their boards. It is also possible that superintendents identify their own performance with that of their boards.

A common external criticism of many boards is the frequent display of conflict among members and seeming incapacity of boards to exhibit negotiated consensual leadership. Members' different views of the board's role are often at the root of internal difficulties, particularly for urban boards, and the cause of the inability of board members to understand each other's positions. Without reaching some consensus, boards will engage in ever-increasing activities in order to respond to the multiple views of a board's role. A "real life" example will help in understanding this phenomenon.

The board of a very large school district in the Washington, D.C., suburbs determined that it needed a workshop on time management, that such skills would solve many of its problems. But upon further evaluation, it became clear that time management would solve nothing so long as the board could not resolve multiple and conflicting definitions of its role. As a result, meetings and activities proliferated. The board had never discussed its role, nor had the members sought to define priorities for the board's use of time. One of the problems this board encountered in role definition stemmed from the selection process; it is appointed by individual members of a county council from discrete electoral districts within the school district. Some members of the board viewed their role as governing on behalf of the whole county district, while others saw themselves as accountable to their local geographic area and to the individual county supervisor who had appointed them to the board.

Boards in the IEL self-assessment sample rated themselves moderately effective in the decisionmaking process. However, the types of decisions boards spend most of their time and energy debating have led to a great deal of criticism, substantiated by a study in West Virginia. In response to a request from the West Virginia legislature's Oversight Commission on Education Accountability (H.C.R. 30), a study of the kinds of decisions and the nature of actions taken by local school boards was carried out as part of a larger study of the effectiveness of local education governance in that state. In this two-part study, the authors analyzed the responses of the twenty-seven boards that had participated in the IEL self-assessment program. Then, a sample of local school board minutes taken from 1985 to 1990 across all fifty-five West Virginia school districts was analyzed. Decisions and actions were organized into ten categories: finance; personnel; permissions (for field trips, attendance at professional meetings, and so forth); presentations to the board (public and staff); students; executive sessions; awards/recognition; policy development and oversight; textbooks and curriculum; legal issues; and "other." While West Virginia school boards rated themselves highest in the area of decisionmaking, the second part of the study discovered that across the fifty-five-board sample, boards spent only 3 percent of their time on decisions about educational policy development and oversight, and 2 percent of their decisions related to textbooks and curriculum. As John Carver notes in his summary report and recommendations to the West Virginia legislature, by any stretch of kindness in interpretation of the data, school boards in that state are dysfunctional. Carver also states that there is no reason to be timid about extrapolating the West Virginia data to school boards in general. Indeed, the IEL data confirm Carver's judgment.

Differences among Urban, Suburban, Small-Town, and Rural Boards

The IEL data indicate more similarities than differences in perceptions of effectiveness among boards governing different types of school districts. However, rural, small-town, and suburban boards rated themselves consistently higher in most assessment categories. This is not surprising. These boards are generally operating in less contentious political environments and can govern with assumptions about greater commonality among constituent values and expectations for education. Many observers of school boards believe that the "caliber" of school board members has declined across all districts in the past decade. However, board members in the suburban, rural, and small-town school districts are still much more apt to come from traditional leadership strata in their areas, participants in the local economic and social power structures with broad community or other leadership experience.

Proponents of education reform and governance restructuring may believe that risk taking and leadership for change are sorely lacking in the rural and small-town school districts, and possibly in the suburbs as well. The reality is that these boards are, relatively speaking, fairly effective, and their performance has not engendered a hue and cry about local governance in their communities, as has happened in large cities. Further, nonurban boards govern in communities where common local values and community characteristics are most jealously protected. Residents of districts like these show no reticence in exerting influence on their state legislators to preserve the status quo. In many of these districts, education is the dominant function in the public sector, accounting for the majority of local government expenditures. In the more well known, affluent suburbs around the country, it is not uncommon for education to account for 70 percent of total local public expenditures. These are the school districts with political clout resulting from the power of their well-off residents and the proportionate share of state tax revenue they yield. Superior educational achievement of students is taken for granted, and the separation of the control of education from other political pressures is a near-religion in these communities.

SCHOOL BOARDS AND SUPERINTENDENTS

The effectiveness of school boards is, in large measure, determined by the character of the board-superintendent relationship. IEL's board self-assessment data indicate that boards frequently fail to avoid involvement in the administration of their districts and do not consider the board-superintendent relationship as part of the superintendent's evaluation. These boards viewed themselves as particularly ineffective in putting into place processes for managing conflict between the board and the superintendent. This is a telling finding in light of the decreasing tenure among superintendents generally, and the acute problem of turnover in large cities.

Tension between school boards and their superintendents is neither new nor surprising; tension is inherent in any lay governing board/professional CEO relationship. Boards of trustees and university or college presidents have growing concerns about their relationship, as do boards of directors and executive directors of voluntary and not-for-profit organizations. Lay board members, irrespective of the type of organization, institution, or agency, frequently come to their positions with minimal understanding of the policy role of the board or the role and authority of an individual board member. Unlike public school systems, in many organizations problems in role definition can be worked out quietly, free from public exposure.

Tension permeates the school board-superintendent relationship. The board governs on behalf of the people, who expect it to reflect their values and expectations for public education and to prevent the excesses of administrative zeal by the professional staff. The tension here is supposed to be constructive. But boards and their superintendents do not operate in a vacuum—increasingly, they play out their different roles while buffeted by high levels of strident and conflicting external demands.

Superintendents' professional education perpetuates the myth that superintendents administer school systems and boards only make policy; in fact, policy and administration have become gray areas with the increasing complexity of public education and shifting constituent expectations. Most board members know they are supposed to set policy, but they also know that boards are legally responsible for everything that occurs, or fails to occur, in their school districts. Neither boards nor superintendents pay sufficient attention to the need to work at developing their relationship to adjust to new demands and the fraying of the boundaries of responsibility. In the major urban districts, the relationship appears more and more to have two stages: the honeymoon with a new superintendent, when all seems possible, and the divorce, when one or the other becomes frustrated enough to terminate the relationship.

The Rise of the Superintendency

Prior to 1900, schools were governed by local boards of education, with guidance provided by charismatic social reformers rather than educational managers. In 1837, the Buffalo city council was the first to appoint a superintendent of common schools, and by 1860, twenty-seven urban school districts had superintendents. The establishment of a central administrative authority, a superintendent, was characteristic of urban schools only at this time, and was not common in rural and small-town schools until the twentieth century. In the less populous school districts, still frequently comprising a one-room schoolhouse, administration of local education remained a manageable option for members of local boards.

The second half of the nineteenth century marked a rapid change from an agricultural to an industrial economy. This industrial progress, accompanied by rapid urban growth and social, ethnic, and economic changes in American culture, put many new demands on society and presented a strong rationale for a more bureaucratized governance structure in all services, including health, safety, charity, and education. The governance of education in urban schools, still modeled after school governance in small towns, was inadequate to meet the new and complex needs of diverse city schoolchildren. The numbers and qualifications of teaching staff, more complex curriculum, and school management itself were all new issues. School board members, in their capacity as volunteers, did not have the expertise or the time to address these burgeoning needs. Schools therefore lagged behind the progress of other developing public service agencies.

Education reformers at the turn of this century, impressed with the accomplishments of business and responsive to the growing belief in scientific management, turned to the corporate world for an organizational model of governance. The structure of school systems, the reformers believed, should correspond to that of large corporations and, following this line of thinking, it was essential to place the power and the control of the schools in one person, the superintendent.

During this period, the roles of individual urban superintendents differed greatly as each one struggled to define the parameters of administrative authority within newly emerging forms of urban government. Tyack refers to the superintendency as being "surrounded by the Horatio Alger myth at the turn of the century."[4] The early literature on school administration discusses the leader as "not only the trained expert, but the free-ranging creator, the crusader who inspired his organizational followers. Was the superintendent a man on a white horse, or a man on one end of the telephone?"[5]

The early-twentieth-century consolidation of school control vested in a handful of local leaders of business and the subsequent merger of ward-based schools in the cities into districtwide systems reinforced the alliance of superintendents with leaders of industry and the development of the hierarchical and bureaucratic structure of school administration. School boards until the 1960s generally exercised their governance authority with the "trusteeship" notion of governing for the whole district at a hands-off distance from operation of the schools. During the era of relative peace in school governance, superintendent tenures of fifteen years and more were not uncommon. Superintendents moved to advance their careers, and, for many, the pinnacle of the career ladder was a city superintendency. The halcyon days of urban superintendents ended with the withdrawal of community "elites" from school board service in the 1960s and the enhanced political power of the historically powerless, who began to confront superintendents and school boards with the failure of schools to respond to the needs of their children.

The School Board-Superintendent Relationship

Perhaps no single issue has had the power of the board-superintendent relationship to compel national attention to focus on local education governance. Issues surrounding this lay-professional relationship have developed since the counterreforms in governance starting in the 1960s, coalescing around the unprecedented vacancies in urban superintendencies featured in the last months of 1990 and first several months of 1991. The number of urban districts involved in searches for superintendents increased to as many as twenty-four in early 1991. The causes for the turnover were many. But in the majority of cases, school boards initiated their superintendents' departures. In some districts, superintendents wearied of the seemingly insoluble educational and political problems besetting their districts or simply could not work in a positive relationship with their boards and moved on to other districts, or left the superintendency. In many of these cases, the school board and the community watched their superintendent's departure with genuine regret. In one urban district, the superintendent, a person with an impeccable national reputation, left a city whose board met 172 times in one year to become the superintendent in a large suburban district. In one of the nation's largest cities, the superintendent quit to enter the private sector, taking leave of the almost insuperable problems facing the school district and a board that functioned more as nine individual school boards than as a nine-person governing body.

However much some critics of school boards may despair over the governing behaviors of urban boards or individual members, many that terminated their superintendent's contract did so with fairly substantial evidence that the superintendent could not or, for a variety of internal political reasons, would not provide effective professional leadership and organizational management to reform the school system. Many of these financially pressed school boards felt so strongly that they bought out remaining years of their superintendents' contracts at costs of over $200,000.

All of these urban boards are discovering in their superintendent searches that the pool of possible candidates is not filled with the "stars" of yesteryear, and the "stars" still in the urban superintendency are either about to retire or will not move, regardless of inducements, from their current districts. With the few exceptions of superintendents coming up through the ranks or coming in from elsewhere, the nation's urban boards are merely rearranging the deck chairs on the *Titanic*. At best, the school boards are, according to Floretta McKenzie, a former superintendent in Washington, D.C., "involved in a game of national musical chairs of applicants"[6] in which the average tenure of superintendents among the forty-five largest urban school districts is now less than three years. Many of these school boards are going to settle for the best of what is available. Ira W. Kinsky, a Los Angeles consultant who conducts superintendent searches for many urban boards, says that "boards increasingly may have to take a chance on hiring somebody long on potential, and maybe a little short on demonstrated performance."[7]

Defining the root problem in the urban superintendency depends, to some extent, on where one stands. It lies in large measure in shortcomings in both boards' and superintendents' performance in their roles and in their capacities to develop effective working relationships. It also springs from the enormity of the pressures on both parties to improve the educational attainment of students who are among the most difficult to teach and whose noneducational needs may be critical determinants of school success. Pressures for visible short-term improvements in educational outcomes are exacerbated by the increasing division of the body politic in the cities, each faction pushing its own recommendations. Add to this the seemingly immovable bureaucratic organizations peopled by principals and teachers who will stay on to outlast board after board and superintendent after superintendent and the tumult in urban superintendencies is not surprising. Communities vent their frustration by turning over the school boards, school boards seek solutions by changing the superintendents, and superintendents express their frustration by leaving.

In most of the nation's 15,000-plus school districts, the school boards and their superintendents play out their respective roles with little more than the inherent tensions between a professional executive and a representative governing board. In these school districts, largely the rural and small-town districts and, to some extent, the affluent and highly homogeneous suburban districts, when superintendents leave it is usually to further their careers in larger or more challenging districts. There are rural school districts where superintendency tenures of fifteen to twenty years or more are not unknown. According to IEL's 1986 study, school board turnover is also lowest in the rural and small-town school districts, where board tenure of more than fifteen years is not uncommon. Continuity in school board membership thus correlates well with superintendents' longevity. But the urban districts may be a harbinger for the others. By the late 1980s, over a third of all school board members nationally were changing each year. This increase in turnover cannot be attributed solely to the school boards in large cities, since these districts account for only about 4 percent of the nation's school districts. The smaller districts in rural areas, small towns, and many of the suburbs are nevertheless more apt to experience continuity in the governing philosophy of new board members and in the expectations held among their more homogeneous communities. Regardless of the quality of the educational leadership in these communities, they start out with a critical advantage in the reforming process due to the stability in the top professional leadership.

IEL's 1986 study findings and those from a study at the Ohio State University[8] indicate that there is no one type of board-superintendent relationship that should be prescribed. Board-superintendent relationships that work depend on the nature of each party's conduct of its role, the condition of the district, the dynamics of community relations, and other political and environmental variables. The culture of each party's role is also important in individual school districts: if boards or superintendents are playing their roles "out of sync" with respect to the variables just described and if they are not consciously aware of how their actions affect the interplay between them, breakdown most likely will occur. Conflict resolution processes are seriously underdeveloped.

Perspectives on the Board-Superintendent Relationship

Robert Peterkin, who stepped down from the Milwaukee superintendency to lead a new administrator training program at the Harvard University Graduate School of Education, observed that, at this point, urban school boards spend little time focused on academic performance but involve themselves in "unbelievably detailed administrative issues related to how the system is run and, very often, who gets jobs."[9] Peterkin and fellow authors Oliver Brown and Leonard Finkelstein also note in an article appearing in *Education Week* that to this situation "a heavy dose of pure, energy-draining politics" may be added, with the result that neither the superintendent nor the board gives adequate attention to priority educational goals and performance assessment.[10]

Paul Houston, who left the superintendency in Tucson, Arizona (at his initiative and with the regret of the community and the board), states, "I think there should be some limitations as to what a board's role is," citing the 172 times the Tucson board met in 1990, approving everything from student field trips to faculty travel.[11] John Dow, superintendent in New Haven, Connecticut, likens the behavior of school board members to assuming the roles of the superintendent, with the result that "you end up in some cases with three or four superintendents, rather than several policymakers and one chief executive."[12]

Lillian Barna, superintendent in Tacoma, Washington, points out that the trend to elect school board members to represent specific districts within a city has resulted in greatly increased politicization of boards. "It has created a turf situation where board members have a tendency to look out for the interest of a particular area they are representing, they fail to see the broader issues."[13] Barna harks back to her previous experience in Albuquerque, New Mexico, where she was hired by a seven-member board elected at large; after the state passed a law requiring that boards be elected by districts, the entire school board was defeated. She resigned soon after, seeing the "writing on the wall."[14]

The characteristics of those serving on school boards, the performance of boards, and the politicization of governance are all offered by superintendents as causes for trouble in their work. Superintendents also cite problems of the superintendency itself when they analyze the major problems that affect the board-superintendent relationship and the effectiveness and longevity of superintendents, particularly in urban districts.

In an IEL telephone interview survey of veteran superintendents in large districts, superintendents in smaller districts, and aspiring superintendents, the issue of working with school boards surfaced as one of the major problems.[15] However, responses to the survey and meetings with urban superintendents indicate that the difficulties stem from the institution of the superintendency as well as from school boards. There was consensus among those surveyed by IEL concerning the inadequacy of current and past preparation for the superintendency and the lack of developmental and support mechanisms for those in the job. The following are illustrative comments of those interviewed:

"We must look at brand new ways of preparing urban school leaders; we don't know how, and university programs are irrelevant."

"Probably the most important thing is not to take a degree in administration."

"Deficits in academic training include not enough help understanding organizational theory and dynamics; weak focus on leadership and leadership issues."

"Human relations skills and conflict management skills are vital."

"It is a political position [the superintendency], yet decidedly nonpolitical course work [was] provided."

"There's nothing about social organizations [in preparation]—the nature and culture of bureaucracies and how to change them."

"We need human relations skills to build coalitions, to work with the board, with the community, with parents."

"Among [the] biggest problem[s]—dealing with collaboration, this is something new and we have no training or support in this."

"Written and oral communications are a problem in dealing with the board and others."

"Need extensive component in training on working with school boards."

"Need educational leaders with broadly gauged backgrounds; broad knowledge, interpersonal skills and strong background in organizational development."

"A major problem is knowing how to respond and be receptive to all diverse groups in the community. Each interest group has its own agenda—need help in problem-solving; with conflict resolution; good communications skills."[16]

These observations provide evidence that both parties, boards and superintendents, contribute to the problems besetting the relationship.

There has been much in the media recently about the relationship drawing on talks with sitting and former superintendents, along with academics, national education observers, and school board watchers. There is far less commentary from school board members. But, if the adage that actions speak louder than words holds true, the number of school boards not renewing contracts, firing superintendents in the midst of contracts, and involving themselves more and more in the running of school districts may provide all the commentary necessary from boards. School boards, with rare exceptions, hire superintendents in whom they have vested confidence and high hopes. In the large urban school districts, the distressing frequency of breakdowns in the relationship that belie these hopes may signal that both parties are in increasing trouble owing to the complexity of both the educational challenges and the political environments. R. David Hall, president of the Washington, D.C., Board of Education, comments that "school boards are like shock absorbers that are expected to respond to all of the problems facing urban communities." He suggests that a new "managerial partnership" may be needed between boards and their superintendents to avoid "superintendents' becoming the fall guys and boards the scapegoats."[17] Thomas Shannon, executive director of the National School Boards Association, says that the controversy in the city districts has at its source the differences among competing constituents; by inference, the battle between boards and their superintendents simply reflects these differences.[18]

Theodore Kolderie of the Center for Policy Studies in St. Paul, Minnesota, suggests in an informal observation that the increasingly political and "intrusive" behavior of boards regarding managerial and administrative matters in the cities may be a consequence of boards' greater responsiveness to the real politics of their communities than superintendents'. Perhaps superintendents are not sufficiently politically attuned to demands for change.

School board members in IEL's studies frequently pointed to the issues of information access and information flow as a cause of problems that gradually erode the relationship. Superintendent behavior that evoked complaint included "burying us in information." The possibility that this is a strategy to keep the board busy was not lost on board members. Members also cited unevenness of the information flow to those who serve on the board, with the "group always supporting the superintendent" getting more information or quicker action on requests than those who frequently opposed or questioned superintendent positions or proposals. Board members' complaints also extended to the superintendent's practice of "counting the votes" and disregarding the minority viewpoints.

Many big-city or big suburban county districts have established staff positions reporting directly to the board. Since this has the obvious potential to create problems with superintendents and school district staff, the question arises as to why this practice is growing. Board members' answers often connote a lack of trust in the type or amount of information a board believes the superintendent or other staff provides in addressing the specific concerns of the board. These boards also feel that the work of board members is so complex and demanding that they must have staff.

Improving the Relationship

The majority of the difficulties in the board-superintendent relationship are behavioral, as documented in a 1986 study by T. E. Davidson,[19] and are, therefore, within the control of one or both parties. Unfortunately, behaviors causing conflict, such as board involvement in micro details of the operations of school districts, appear to be increasing, and the will or understanding necessary to control them seem in decline. Meanwhile, communities increasingly elect persons to school boards to represent narrow constituent or issue interests who, much more than in the past, have not proved their capacity for broad community leadership.

School boards and superintendents can improve the possibilities for productive working relationships. However, both parties will have to be forthright and decide that negotiating, developing, and sustaining the relationship is a core responsibility of both parties. Neither superintendent candidates nor school boards really anticipate stresses on the relationship from stated or implied objectives like "We want someone who will clean out the 'dead wood' in the system." Superintendent candidates might usefully take a board through some simulations of the consequences of such a board directive and determine how the board might respond to political fallout from it.

The euphoria that attends completion of a superintendent search and starting anew appears to overwhelm common sense about investing in development of the relationship. In the first year, time should be devoted regularly to solid dialogue, and "checkpoints" in the new relationship should be set up to take care of any trouble signs. Continuous attention to the relationship ought to be a high priority. School boards should also be willing to invest in consultative support for a new superintendent. Boards in almost all cities and many suburbs spend anywhere from $25,000 to $100,000 for superintendent searches. Supporting a new superintendent is no less worthy an expenditure.

School boards and superintendents need to anticipate issues that could cause stress in their relationship rather than react to crises. Boards should take the initiative to assure there is constant sorting of policy and administrative roles, yet both parties have to learn to live with ambiguities in their roles. Boards and superintendents should establish mutually agreed processes for resolving conflicts. Boards should also incorporate a mutual evaluation of the board-superintendent relationship in their annual evaluation of the superintendent.

INSTITUTIONAL PROBLEMS OF SCHOOL BOARDS

Many of the problems of school boards arise, to a great extent, from the nature of the institution as a representative governing body. Problems also stem from the delegation by the states of total responsibility to school boards with very little guidance about what it means to be responsible without being involved in everything that occurs in a school district. School boards contend with public misunderstanding of the role of boards and the apathy evidenced by the low voter turnout in school board elections, as well as increased difficulty in securing candidates for school boards who have the experience, skills, and longer-term vision required. Additionally, boards are affected by inherent tensions arising from their dual mission to govern responsively on behalf of the current interests and demands of the adults who elect them and the present and future interests of the students.

School Boards and Their Publics

School boards across the nation, depending on the type of community, are variously accused of being "rubber stamps" for their superintendents, adversaries of their superintendents, profligate in the name of education, politicians furthering their own interests at the expense of students, a closed group that listens to no one, or a collection of individuals who respond to narrow constituencies and provide little district leadership. On the other hand, school boards are perceived in some communities as a group of individuals seeing to it that the kind of education the community wants for its children is provided in the schools. School boards can be all of these things depending upon what a citizen expects of the schools, believes is the role of an elected or appointed representative body, holds as standards for elected officials' behavior, defines as her or his community. A citizen's experience, education, and breadth of perspective also contribute to the assessment of the board.

The evidence from national opinion polls shows, time after time, that while respondents may think education is in trouble, they do not, with the exception of larger urban districts, believe "their" schools are bad—in fact, those polled generally rate schools in their own communities with a grade of A or B. This obviously does not mean that all are satisfied with their schools in these communities, but it does give a fair indication, despite public support reported in the polls for some kind of national standards or examinations, that the average citizen is not up in arms about the quality of education where it is felt most directly. The business elite may be outraged, along with academics, governors, and national policymakers, but the general public is not. Therefore, while criticism of the school board may be a favorite town sport in many school districts across the nation, there must be reasons other than the quality of education.

There is despair in the major urban districts, however. The boards in these districts epitomize the problems of representative democracy when publics, including large populations of the historically disenfranchised seeking to redress the skewed distribution of public resources, are divided and have no mechanisms for compromise and for developing community priorities. Even in the suburbs, small towns, and rural communities, though, school boards must frequently deal with differences that can erupt into highly charged emotional issues dividing or toppling board members. One has only to look to the politics of curricula and textbooks, with school boards consumed by the "liberal" vs. "conservative" and the "creationist" vs. "evolutionist" pressures, to begin to understand one of the basic problems for boards—each of us believes that our representatives should represent *us*. On whose behalf do the boards govern—the students? The adults who support the schools through local and state taxes? The state, which views education in terms of broader interests? The economic power structure? While in theory there is a confluence of long-term interests among all of the above, this is not always discernible to all parties. We are far from consensus on how education can be structured and supported to respond to all these interests.

American Distrust of Intellectualism

Any analysis of school boards and their performance as a representative governing body must take into account an American reality that explains both why school boards have not been in the forefront of leadership for a new era of heightened intellectual attainment and why there has been no great hue and cry about the leadership of public education: there is a basic anti-intellectual streak in the American psyche. At some level, Americans equate intellectual achievement with elitism. As with other dichotomies in the American psyche—a belief that we are "rugged individualists" and yet naturally cooperate to help each other—we have not reconciled our rhetoric about the importance of education with our deeply rooted distrust of "intellectuals." We believe in enough education for our children to achieve as much as we, or perhaps more, but we do not endorse scholarship enthusiastically. Programs for intellectually and artistically talented children and adolescents are often resented by other parents and even by professional staff in schools. The most visible accolades in most high schools go to athletes, not to superior academic achievers. In a small school district in Mississippi, a student was named a semifinalist in the National Merit Scholarship competition—the first student so named from this district in twenty years—an accomplishment noted in the back pages of the local newspaper. One of the school's athletic victories was front-page news the same day.

The American public hears but does not yet understand that the work of the future—the world for which schools are preparing students—will be much more dependent on intellectual skills and that the fruit of one's labor will be shaped by the head more than the hands. Irrespective of the governance structure of American public education, there will be no great leaps in support for intellectual achievement and for schooling that cultivates the mind in addition to teaching the "three R's" until there is a broad shift in public attitudes toward learning.

Demographic Changes

Two major demographic phenomena have occurred since the middle of this century that make the governance tasks of school boards more complex and difficult. The student population has become increasingly diverse, and more children come from populations historically more difficult to educate due to their economic and social circumstances. This demographic change has had a particular impact on the major urban school districts. The majority of these districts' students are from economically disadvantaged families and racial and ethnic minorities. School boards in the increasingly diverse communities are attempting to educate students whose life situations and developmental deficiencies prior to entering school are, in large measure, determinants affecting success in school. In addition, many school boards are governing districts that have had heavy influxes of immigrants; some districts are struggling to provide appropriate education to over one hundred linguistic and ethnic minority populations.

School boards also are contending with the erosion of the natural political base for public education. Across the nation, only 20–25 percent of households have children of public school age. In some cities, the figure is as low as 15 percent. Together with the increasing minority presence in city schools, this demographic shift calls into question the ability of urban school boards to muster the strength necessary to keep revenues flowing into education in their districts at a time of tremendous need.

American Expectations for the "Quick Fix"

Most school boards want immediate improvement in educational attainment for the students in their districts as much as their constituents. School boards know, however, even as they publicly demand a fast turnaround from professional staff, that substantive organizational change and major improvements in student achievement require more time than either politicians or their constituents will tolerate. As a people, we tend to rush to identify the problem and search for a quick fix. The problems for education are neither simple nor amenable to quick fixes. We ignore that the public schools declined over time and are the victim, in many respects, of our putting our heads in the sand about how the world was changing economically and politically.

School boards are political bodies, and the members of political bodies like to tell their constituents that problems can be fixed. There is great disillusionment and anger when results cannot be seen quickly. But how do you tell the voters, "Elect me to a three-year term of office, and in ten years you may see change in the institution"? Pressures for change on school boards are then translated into frequently unreasonable demands on superintendents, who are hardly in a position to object on grounds of feasibility. A little realistic dialogue between school boards and constituents is long overdue.

CHAPTER 4

THE FUTURE OF LOCAL EDUCATION GOVERNANCE: STRATEGIES FOR REFORM AND OPTIONS FOR CHANGE

In the near future, the majority of the nation's schools will continue to be governed by locally elected (95 percent of school boards are elected) lay governing boards. This political reality makes it imperative to consider seriously how these elected boards can be reformed to make them more effective in governance and in providing leadership for public education. The first section of this chapter focuses on strategies for strengthening and reforming local lay governance. Some reform suggestions might be suitable to local introduction, but in some instances state action would be required to support local initiatives, or to put in place changes in the current governance structure. Many astute observers of education governance as it is currently practiced believe that radical change in public education governance is imperative—particularly in the beleaguered cities, where there are so few positive results from a decade of attempts to reform and restructure public schooling. In the second section of this chapter, several ideas for more radical governance change are discussed.

REFORMS FOR SCHOOL BOARDS

There are reform strategies at our disposal to attack some of the more egregious problems affecting school boards as currently constituted. Some of them might seem intrusive to those within the school board community; admittedly, some would impose standards for school board service and specific requirements of boards that neither the nation nor states demand of other elected representative governing bodies. However, since the state constitutions and state legislation control the governance of education, there is nothing to prohibit states, barring a loss on appeal to state courts, from implementing any of the suggestions other than the political currency that would have to be expended.

Improvement of Qualifications for School Board Service

States can establish criteria for persons who seek election or appointment to school boards. Such criteria might range from some set level of educational attainment, for example, high school graduation, to a required orientation session for potential candidates and substantive training for persons elected or appointed to boards. Orientation might incorporate not only an overview of the roles and responsibilities of school boards and individual members, but also simulations followed by assessments of candidates' ability in the policy development process, analysis of educational issues, interpersonal skills, and understanding of educational issues in the community, state, and nation. A state might stop short of denying board service to a potential candidate who does not participate in or "pass" the orientation, but the results could be made known to the public. This approach is basically a certification for the practice of governance, and while without precedent in this country, the times may call for dramatic action.

Selection panels for school board candidates are not without precedent. Some communities have established citizen panels that recruit and screen candidates for the board of education. Candidates are endorsed through these panels, and information about the candidates is widely disseminated to the voters. The political problems that have arisen around this process usually lie in perceptions that particular strata of the citizenry control the process and that unstated criteria are used in endorsement. The history of such candidate selection panels and, indeed, the current resurgence of organized education interest groups in some of the major cities that employ citizen panels tend to confirm that particular interests certainly have a strong influence upon these community nominating bodies. The end result may be positive for education governance, but care should be exercised to assure credible representation in any organized nominating process. A broad and representative method of choice needs to be instituted just to determine membership on the selection panel itself. This would put grass roots debate at the beginning of the selection process for school board members, rather than after they are seated.

In the history of governance reform, one of the most enduring selection panels was the Cincinnati Citizens School Committee (CSC) mentioned in an earlier chapter, which controlled the membership of the Cincinnati School Board and public education in that city from the early 1920s until the late 1960s.[1] But instituting candidate selection panels does not have to mean control by a few. There is a resurgence of business leaders and other civic elites organizing to nominate slates for school board elections; even so, these recent efforts (Detroit and St. Louis are examples) reflect an understanding that nominees for the school board must reflect community diversity. The elites themselves are not usually on the slates.

Election of School Boards through Political Parties

The majority of school boards in this nation are chosen in nonpartisan elections held in the spring or summer. This manner of electing school boards dates back to the urban governance reforms of the early twentieth century, which sought to remove education governance from the more damaging impacts of local politics. Nonpartisan elections served the objectives of those elites that were fundamentally behind the turn-of-the-century reforms. This echelon of civic-minded patricians had no need to connect to political parties or municipal or county officeholders in order to retain power and shape the schools. They were accountable to themselves alone, needing endorsement from none but their peers.

Today, however, removal from the organization and accountability, however minimal, afforded by political parties has resulted in the isolation of school board members, so that they generally have much weaker power bases than do other officeholders in their communities. Once on a school board, members must constantly play up their work and their positions with the voters to sustain individual constituencies. The political parties in turn can wash their hands of any responsibility for one of the community's major public institutions—an institution upon which the economic and social viability of cities may well depend.

Electing school board members by partisan election does not necessarily mean a return to the abuses of the late nineteenth century. There is nothing to preclude establishing citizen advisory nominating committees to work with the political parties in seeking and endorsing school board nominees. Further, the political primary election is alive and well in this land. Candidates who might seek but be denied nomination would then have an electoral recourse to press their candidacy.

Partisan school board elections do not necessarily mean political party control of school board members, as is commonly feared. Connecticut, with rare exceptions, has partisan elections for school board and other town government offices. The involvement of the parties with their school board members varies from almost none after election to an expectation that priority positions of a party will be reflected in a board member's voting. The difference has to do with the political culture of each community, not with the fact that school boards are elected in partisan fashion. For example, the author was an elected school board member in a Fairfield County community and rarely heard from her political party. In a similar community in the same county, school board members experience very direct pressure from their political parties.

Almost all possible changes that might be undertaken to shore up school boards have potential downsides because we simply cannot know in advance how each will play out. Any proposed reform must be considered in terms of current governance problems and the potential for a particular change or combination of changes to overcome them. There could be a replay of the excesses of political control of school boards. But we know that the current process does not prevent the politicization of school board members, particularly in the cities, or polarization around certain issues. Further, in those cities that vote school boards by discrete electoral districts, the behavior is very similar to that which was so abhorred in the old urban ward system. Board members tend to respond to their individual constituencies, and there is no communitywide structure holding them accountable or bringing them together. At the very least, political parties cut across their communities and, therefore, have a vested interest in the collective behavior of their officeholders. If urban school boards were elected by political party, mayors, city/county council members, judges (where these are elected), and state representatives and senators from the urban districts would have some common cause with those who govern education. Moving to partisan elections would at least dispel the myth that education is not political and that it is removed from political pressures in the cities.

Linkage of Education and General Purpose Government

School boards and their professional employees have long contended that the schools cannot "do everything," but increasingly the schools are looked to as the locus for solving problems and providing services that society, or state legislatures, deem important for children and adolescents. In many instances, schools themselves have initiated services in the face of the overwhelming needs of their students—needs that interfered with learning. Urban school districts and poor rural districts, along with some of their aging suburban counterparts, are facing incredible challenges arising from the demographics of their student populations. Children and adolescents from families unable to meet their most basic needs have become the majority in many urban districts. As the extent of neediness grows beyond the capacity of the schools to cope, the larger community must begin to accept responsibility for the totality of the issues that determine the welfare of students, and directly affect their success in school and their entry into adulthood.

However, there are few established structures at the local level that encourage dialogue or action among the providers of education and other human services—in fact, many disincentives exist in the form of categorical regulation and financing of services. The deliberate distancing of education from other governmental functions works to the detriment of children in crisis in the latter part of this century. Even in those cities and counties where the school board is appointed by the mayor or county council, the political relationship has not produced systematic communication, planning, or coordination to meet the needs of children and their families.

Desperate people will begin to consider change, and we are now beginning to see some initiatives at the national level. Translating the rhetoric into action at the local level, however, remains problematic. Several national organizations (the National School Boards Association, American Association of School Administrators, National League of Cities, National Association of Counties, International City Management Association, and National Association of Towns and Townships) participated in a conference in February 1991 to discuss collaborative approaches for the delivery of services to children. These groups developed a joint statement calling for a greater commitment by all government agencies to meeting the needs of children and youth. They intend to undertake joint legislative proposals, adopt organizational policies that encourage collaboration, and develop strategies for their local constituents.

Actually, these national organizations are following, not leading, their constituents, many of whom are already convinced that they must do something radically different for the children and families in their communities. Like spring, collaboration is breaking out all over the states and localities, but it tends to be focusing on more of the same in service delivery, or is project-oriented. If improved services for children and their families are going to be anything but "the luck of the draw" depending on where people live and the commitment and ability of policymakers and administrators in office at a particular time, then serious attention needs to be given to new policy and management structures for these services—structures that will bring all those with any responsibility for children and their families together and make them mutually accountable.

A total revolution in the governance structure of human services will be a long time, if ever, in coming. In the meantime, there are measures that can be taken to assure cooperation and communication between education and other human and social services. The states, which determine the responsibilities and roles of school boards, could explicitly require joint assessment and planning for children's needs, jointly developed goals, and mutual accountability among agencies. The majority of states already require school boards to develop goals and objectives and to report regularly on progress; it makes little sense to exclude children's personal and social needs from these reports and plans. Success would require that the states "get their act together" so that the other human services could work coherently with education.

Existing political and bureaucratic systems have few incentives to change even slightly. Nevertheless, states can take steps to assist school districts and local governments, along with the nonprofit community organizations that deliver many social services, in voluntary efforts to work together. Incentives could be provided in the form of regulatory relief from state laws and regulations (as well as promises to pursue federal regulatory relief) and increased or redirected state resources. Some states are already providing waivers to encourage local coordination. Given the difficulties reported by those in the localities, probably the most important support states can offer these voluntary collaborative efforts is to provide additional funding or to direct some resources in agency budgets to support the necessary changes in organizational and staff behavior.[2] All involved, from elected officeholders to the professionals directly engaged in providing services, have to change how they view success in their job, the role of their organizations or agencies, and their professional identification. This is hard work, but without these changes there will be no basic improvement in meeting children's and families' needs.

School Board Assessment and Development

Several ideas have been put forth thus far about strategies that, however modest, do call for changes that would have a fairly dramatic impact upon school boards—strategies to improve the talent for school board service, to go back, particularly in the cities, to electing boards through the political parties, and to bridge the isolation of education from regular government. These changes address some of the more obvious problems that harm governance effectiveness, but they will not solve the problem of the basic capacity of school boards to govern, particularly in complex political and social environments that exert pressures on boards. We can no longer rely on an implicit belief that persons elected to office can exercise public authority effectively because they have been chosen democratically and are therefore accountable to the citizenry. In fact, such a small percentage of the electorate bothers to vote in school board elections (10–15 percent, according to national averages) that it would be difficult for any member or board as a whole to assume approval of performance or any kind of mandate for action.

School boards' neglect of their performance and development has been well documented in the IEL data, the experience of outsiders working with boards, and the reports of the state school boards associations.[3] Currently, there is growing acceptance of board self-evaluation and awareness of the need to deal with the more serious problems of conflict-ridden boards or boards that find themselves at the center of community controversy. However, past and present experience teaches that most boards seek help only when problems are already acute. Further, boards that regularly pay attention to honing their leadership abilities are usually those with the fewest problems. Urban boards, in the IEL experience, are most resistant to spending time on assessing their performance and committing to regular developmental activities.

Eight states now require training for new board members, and Kentucky requires some ongoing training for all board members. But these efforts are so minimal (in Kentucky, eighteen hours for new board members and six for other board members) and so tightly focused on individual board members that they cannot be termed board development. Several state school boards associations offer orientation programs for newly elected members or appointees prior to their taking office. Participation in these programs is voluntary.

Regular self-assessment and substantive development and training are imperative to improve the governance performance of local boards. For this to occur in the immediate future, states will have to mandate it and include appropriations (perhaps on a sliding scale of ability to pay locally) in legislation. If states truly believe the performance of local governance is related to achieving structural education reforms, then improvements in governance should be accorded equal importance with states' efforts to reform curriculum, testing, and the teaching profession.

A nonlegislated board assessment and development strategy must educate citizens as well as school boards to pay serious attention to the quality of governance. The corporate community should become a source of strong political support; moreover, business investment in improving governance through its expertise in human resources development and organizational change and its financial resources would go a long way toward realizing the objective of systemic reform in public education.

New Labor-Management Models for Discussion and Implementation of Education Reforms

In school districts that operate under state collective bargaining laws (and even in those without, the "meet and confer" states), school boards and their professional employees are locked into an adversarial relationship that controls almost all discussion about issues of concern to either party. Over the years since the first state collective bargaining laws in the 1960s, issues within the scope of collective bargaining have expanded through case law, state statute, and school boards' acquiescence in giving away what had been "management prerogatives" in financial trade-offs with professional unions. The result is that few boards or unions can initiate dialogue about educational issues without the concern that at any time discussion might turn to something that will be interpreted as within the scope of collective bargaining. This is patently dysfunctional for the purposes of mutual decisionmaking on education reforms.

Twelve California school districts are experimenting with Educational Policy Trust Agreements that enable teachers, as represented by their union, and school management to develop agreements on professional issues. These are issues that may be interpreted as outside the traditional scope of collective bargaining or that can be better negotiated in a different structure.[4] The Trust Agreement Project is a cooperative effort of the California Federation of Teachers, the California School Boards Association, the California Teachers Association, and the Association of California School Administrators. The project operates under the auspices of Policy Analysis for California Education (PACE), a university-based research center located in the schools of education at the University of California at Berkeley, Stanford University, and the University of Southern California.

A trust agreement is a written compact between a school district and its teachers represented by their union. These agreements specify educational issues with which teachers and school managers are jointly concerned and establish mechanisms outside the collective bargaining process for dealing with them. "Trust" in these agreements has two meanings. The first is the traditional meaning of "trust," signifying the trusting nature of the relationship that must develop or already exist between the parties. The second meaning corresponds to the legal definition of a trust—the parties set aside resources (time, money, personnel, authority) "in trust" to be used to solve the mutually defined educational problems. Trust agreements also transfer financial resources or authority, or both, from the exclusive control of school boards and district administration either to teachers or to teachers and management acting together.

The hoped-for outcomes are workplace reforms that will improve education in the schools. The pilot test of Educational Policy Trust Agreements expected to demonstrate that it is possible to link labor relations and school reform effectively. Three years after the start of the pilot test, trust agreements appeared to be altering decisionmaking in the demonstration school districts, and teachers and school managers were judged to be assuming greater collective responsibility for educational processes and outcomes.

School districts such as Dade County (Florida), Los Angeles, and Rochester (New York) have received a great deal of national attention as a result of contracts negotiated within traditional collective bargaining structure. Viewed as dramatic "breakthroughs" because they incorporate negotiated agreements pertaining to key reform objectives, the contracts remain vulnerable to conflicts relating to other provisions. Rochester had difficulties in the 1990-91 school year in contract negotiations, which were marked by acrimonious debates about salary increases.

The new trust approach in California is seeking to change the relationship between management and labor for the purposes of achieving mutual objectives. It is not an attempt to subvert unions, nor to remove "noneducational" issues from the traditional collective bargaining process. The experiment bears watching.

STATE ASSISTANCE FOR SCHOOL BOARDS

There are measures that states could initiate both to relieve boards from some of their most time-consuming and hostility-inducing responsibilities and to buttress and strengthen local governance. These suggestions do not require dismantling the basic system of local school boards.

Removal of Boards' Quasi-Judicial Responsibilities

School boards in most states must hear and decide disputes arising among their employees, parents, and citizens. In a large school district, or in a district with contentious labor relations or a very active legal community, local boards find themselves presiding at hearings several times a month. This places the board, intended at least in theory to make policy, in the position of ruling on its own policies. The desirability of this is debatable. Even more harmful is that these rulings consume board time, attract the glare of media attention, and may engender lingering hostility.

States could establish a system of community-based mediation and arbitration panels that would operate under their own authority, and be the ultimate judges of complaints and disputes. Many states already have binding arbitration for the resolution of labor contract negotiations in school districts. Some communities have established mediation and arbitration centers outside the courts for the resolution of disputes that do not arise from criminal acts. States may well stop short of mandating such a system, but with enabling legislation, school districts could test this change in boards' roles.

States might delegate to a local jurisdiction the power to appoint or elect members of such a mediation and arbitration panel, thus preempting the outcry over state control of the resolution of local issues. Interestingly, states that have instituted binding arbitration by state-appointed panels for resolution of collective bargaining in school districts are not experiencing any great pressure to overturn these laws, now that the parties are used to them. The downside, some would say, is that binding arbitration has over time removed the urgency to settle locally from both boards and unions. However, a system of locally determined arbitration panels would ensure that decisions reflect local issues, and local people would be accountable for the effectiveness and efficiency of panel deliberations and decisions.

Collective Bargaining and State Salary Schedules

A more "radical" change from the above suggestion would be to create a system wherein the states institute statewide collective bargaining/conferring to establish salaries, fringe benefits, and basic conditions of employment. The state would set salaries, with variations reflecting differences in cost of living, teaching conditions, education, and experience. Such a strategy might have many salutary effects. Local boards would not be embroiled in contract negotiations (or meeting and conferring in noncollective-bargaining states), the "whipsaw" effect of competing for concessions among neighboring districts in negotiations would be eliminated, and local boards, superintendents, and other administrators would be less consumed with issues arising from the administration of teacher contracts.

The majority of school boards find contract negotiations among the most vexing of their responsibilities. School districts that have experienced strikes find that, even ten years later, the residue from the hostilities continues to affect relations in schools and the collective bargaining process.

Direct Assistance to Strengthen Local Governance

No state, to date, has incorporated a specific governance focus in its plans for reshaping the services provided by its department of education, consistent with the small attention that states have paid to governance at all. School boards would not necessarily embrace such assistance from the states, at least in the beginning, nor do the majority of state departments of education currently have such expertise. But states might, for instance, establish panels of experts in governance who could be referred to school boards needing assistance. To this point, as mentioned earlier, any state action to improve governance is limited to so many hours of "seat time" in school board training for new or sitting board members, with the responsibility for design and delivery of such training passing mainly to the state school boards associations. No state, except for West Virginia, has officially recognized that the real issue in local governance is the performance of boards as corporate governing bodies.

State-Appointed Masters to Assist School Districts

Several states have enacted punitive legislation that allows the state to take over a school district, removing the local board and the superintendent where educational failure is manifest. States with such legislation do have a process that allows time for districts to respond to specific state findings prior to takeover. However, this process is invoked in the most extreme situations, not as an early intervention strategy. The political culture of state and local school district relationships where control is at stake is, to put it as mildly as possible, antagonistic. Moreover, there is little historical indication that state departments of education are capable of providing real assistance beyond exercising their regulatory and punitive authority. Local boards, in general, do not look to the state for help because they are not sure it is there, and they are unwilling to give evidence voluntarily about problems that might bring the state into their affairs.

But a new trend is evident among state departments of education. Parallel to the efforts to make local central school districts more supportive of individual schools, several states are enacting changes in the philosophy and organization of their departments of education to make them supporters and sustainers of local districts' education reform efforts. The state of Virginia not only restructured the department of education but also required all employees there to resign and then reapply for new positions in the reorganized department. Now that Kentucky has a commissioner of education, that state will move ahead with the same strategy, which has been incorporated in state governance reform legislation.

A system of state-selected and state-supported masters could provide sorely needed help to school boards attempting to solve specific problems in their districts. Many school districts need targeted expertise, not a takeover of all district functions. Early intervention makes much greater sense than waiting until a school district is demonstrably dysfunctional. States might identify experts in staff development, curriculum, organizational change, conflict resolution, labor relations, or parent involvement. The masters might be state professional staff (not necessarily from the department of education), national experts, or even superintendents or experienced teachers. Corporations might volunteer staff with appropriate expertise to serve on a state's panel of masters. This would be a significant contribution from the business community.

School boards in well-financed districts routinely bring in consultants when needed. School boards with very limited resources, however much one might think the behavior shortsighted, find it difficult to justify spending resources on outside expertise when struggling just to finance the educational program. Benefits to states would far outweigh costs if resources were expended on early and targeted intervention rather than on a state takeover later.

In very difficult situations, state-appointed masters might go into a school district to direct the problem-solving process and report back to state authorities. School boards would be accountable through the masters to the state. In other circumstances, "voluntary" use of the state master would be similar to hiring a consultant.

State-Local Working Partnerships for Education Reform

It is not lost on school boards that they have been nonplayers in state education reforms. State legislators, rightly or wrongly, have hardly been shy about their lack of confidence in school boards to initiate or achieve education reforms on their own. In fact, some school districts have always exceeded state requirements, setting the standards that drive higher expectations throughout the nation. Beyond these exceptional districts, there are many others that sowed and continue to cultivate major reforms in education. In most states, the well-funded and sophisticated districts as well as the large urban districts have traditionally enjoyed greater expertise on staff than exists at the state level. It is difficult to convince such local districts that all wisdom lies with state legislators or civil servants. State departments of education are subject to the same problems of inertia and resistance to change within their bureaucracies that Chubb and Moe assign to local school district bureaucracies.[5]

Reasonable people will agree that the state-local relationship is nonproductive in terms of reaching states' objectives for improved education standards while sustaining the best elements of local determination. The interdependence of the two levels of educational governance is obvious, but as happens in personal relationships, each is reluctant to be the first to say, "I need you."

States would be well advised to bring local boards (as well as their superintendents) into policy deliberations, the shaping of regulations, and strategy sessions for implementation of state education legislation and nonlegislated reforms. Establishing a true partnership, not just inviting boards to testify individually or through their state associations, would do much not only to diffuse antagonisms, but also, more importantly, to reform education. School boards, if treated as part of the solution, might be eager to cooperate rather than to continue waving the flag for local control. It would be both instructive and productive, for instance, for the education committee of a state legislature to work with local boards on time frames for implementation of legislation.

RADICAL CHANGE IN LOCAL GOVERNANCE

Breakdowns in the governance and leadership of public education in many of the nation's major cities have given impetus to calls for changing the very way in which the nation governs its schools. The formerly unthinkable, abolition of locally elected school boards, has moved out of the realm of academic dialogue and wishful thinking among the cognoscenti, as evidenced by Boston's shift to a mayorally appointed governing body.

While it is true that in many of the nation's urban school districts the governance practices of school boards may be a deterrent to systemic reforms, on the other side of the argument one can point to serious weaknesses in many of those who are in or are likely to assume the superintendency and in the ability of teachers (most of whom had no training in urban education in their formal studies) to function effectively in these districts. Urban environmental factors may, upon closer analysis, be at the root of the governance problems. If a multiethnic and variably affluent citizenry elects a board reflective of its divergent nature to direct a system serving the poorest and least powerful among the population, the result, not surprisingly, is often ineffective governance and leadership for the schools. However, irrespective of the multiplicity of likely causes for the problems of urban education, few would disagree that the effectiveness of governance is central to any investigation of what is wrong.

Two questions should frame any dialogue about basic structural change in the nation's system for governing public education: (1) will another system of governance, in and of itself, produce better outcomes from the schools? and (2) if the considered answer to the first question is yes, is it necessary to change the governance system for all school districts? Politicians will ask themselves one more question, "Is changing the educational governance structure worth the political cost?" In addition, the following caution should be kept in mind when considering radical changes in the governance structure. As a people (professional and nonprofessional, informed and noninformed), Americans have a tendency to look for the "silver bullet." As a consequence, we often shoot a succession of such bullets at complex problems. When each bullet fails to do the job, we discard it and look for the next, refusing to countenance that a fusillade of bullets may be necessary to solve the problem.

The possible structural changes in local governance discussed below fall into two categories: the first preserves some kind of separate policy function for education at the district level yet fundamentally alters the roles of school boards and their scope of responsibilities. The second category of changes would abolish separate local governance or redefine the whole notion of one system of public education.

Restructuring Local Governance

State education laws make boards responsible for everything in their districts from assuring an equal and efficient education for all students to making certain that all students know not only state history but also the state bird and state flower. Boards that operate in the early twentieth-century tradition of reform governance delegate much of the "nuts and bolts" for which state law holds them responsible. The more prevalent board practice, however, is to get involved—out of personal or political inclination, or in response to perceived constituent expectations—in the operations of the district, such as approving all field trips for students, asking for detailed operational reports, confirming all district administrative hirings, ruling on staff participation in professional meetings, and even debating changes in school bus routes and the food served in the cafeterias. Most board members, when confronted with this behavior, will say that their constituents expect it of them. This may be true, but boards do little to change these expectations and to educate their constituents about where a board's efforts should be properly invested. Board members who come onto these micromanaging boards with a very different definition of the board's role frequently serve only one term and, if still motivated to serve public education afterward, work from the outside.

Over time, states have determined the roles and responsibilities of local school boards. They began with what local boards were already doing, and expanded that as local roles and responsibilities grew to meet new challenges as well as the demands posed by the growing involvement of the states in local educational affairs. What the states have defined, the states can redefine.

Local Policy Boards

States might create enabling legislation to allow local jurisdictions to establish a system of local policy boards that could be elected or appointed in school districts for the express purpose of providing public policy forums, determining broad goals, adopting policies to guide a school district toward these goals, and providing policy oversight. The policies of such a board would have authority under the law, thus assuring the accountability to the community of the professionals entrusted with managing the school district. This change in the role of boards would leave the structure of local public school districts intact. School boards would become true policy boards. The board responsible for education policy and oversight and the local unit of general government would have joint stakes in the performance of the school district, and the superintendent's role and accountability would be clarified. A policy board's authority could be expanded to the hiring of the local superintendent; alternatively, the superintendent might be an employee of the local government. This structure would attract, in all probability, very different people to school board service, particularly in the cities, and would allow the board to function as a forum for community discussion of educational issues.

Such policy boards should be required to discuss goals and policies with the units of government responsible for financing the schools. Government could appoint a financial officer responsible for school district financial management who would work alongside the superintendent of schools. As an alternative, the responsibility for educational and financial management could be lodged with the superintendent, who would report to both the education policy board and general government. The local government jurisdiction in each case would employ teachers and administrators and delegate supervision to the superintendent.

Critics will point to possible dangers if those who set policy are not also responsible for adopting budgets consistent with that policy. Others might object that the citizenry would not be able to determine whom to hold accountable for educational outcomes, since the policy board might be apt to say, "We did our job, but local funding, or fiscal management, is preventing us from reaching the goals, or implementing our policies," or something similar. But that is the point. The policy board's responsibilities would be clear and fulfilled if it did its job of setting goals and establishing and monitoring implementation of policies.

Those who fear giving greater autonomy to professional educators will also take issue. But this structure would actually create greater accountability for the professional leadership of the school districts, setting out a clear division of labor and including a role for general government. Today, with both boards and superintendents managing school districts, it is difficult to determine the locus of accountability.

Redefinition of Central Boards vis-a-vis Local Schools

If urban educational reformers are serious about devolving authority and accountability to the local school site, assuring success requires a redefinition by states or, in the best of all possible worlds, local jurisdictions of the role of the central board of education and central administration. The Illinois legislature, pressured by parents, citizens, and the economic power structure in Chicago, legislated a new definition of the authority of the central school board and administration, and that of governance units at the level of the individual school. Improved educational outcomes for students have yet to be demonstrated, and no verdict has been reached determining if critics who say the system has been balkanized, but there is a new governance structure to support the objectives of greater autonomy and accountability at the school level.

Other districts that have made much of moving to school-based management within the current governance structure are facing real barriers resulting from confusion over roles within the district and the reluctance of boards either to give up power or to trust the schools to make decisions. In Los Angeles, both the teacher contract and board policy embrace school-based management and commit the district to reallocation of powers and resources. Yet the central board has instituted a review and approval process that reserves the power to change, approve, or eliminate any "line item" in a school's site management plan. With practically no guidance in how to readjust the scope and latitude of central board responsibilities, it is difficult for those "draining the swamp" to figure out how to stay out of the way of the alligators.

States need to understand that school boards have legitimate concerns about their ultimate liability for what occurs in their districts if they let loose their central control. Boards are also struggling with the reality that the professionals they hire, trained and certified according to state standards and regulations, have not been educated in nor required to demonstrate competencies required for school autonomy. There are many in the education profession who want and are ready for new professional autonomy—and many who are not.

What can be done to enhance the success of school-based management? States, working with cohorts of local boards and superintendents, could develop new policies and regulations that clearly set out the roles and responsibilities of central boards and administrations in districts that offer school-site autonomy. States would hold a board accountable for only strictly delineated actions in support of individual schools, and would determine the extent of individual schools' accountability to the local board. This process would produce some very interesting dialogue among schools, local boards, and state policymakers. At the least, such a process would call for some integration of the conflicting strategies to achieve education reform—mandates from above and empowerment of those closest to the students. Theoreticians may have reconciled these two themes of reform, but the messages are definitely confusing to those who must implement both policy directions in practice.

School Boards as Community Contractors for Educational Services

There are precedents for school boards looking outside the public school system for delivery of educational services. School boards have contracted with private, for-profit organizations for educational programs that are tied to "guarantees" of educational attainment. Florida's Dade County board has contracted with a corporation that is responsible for an entire school. Contracting for educational services allows communities to retain the coherence provided by a governing board responsible for assuring elementary and secondary education within a framework of local goals and objectives and, at the same time, permits flexibility in how education is provided. The local education authority could determine that it will contract for preschool programs with community-based organizations, with local colleges or universities for high school education, even with church-sponsored schools (as Detroit is considering in its choice/voucher plan), so long as constitutional requirements are not violated.

This option, while radical, still stops short of disbanding a local system for public education. There would continue to be a policy board determining the local goals, broad policy framework, and accountability standards. This board might continue to operate schools, or it could phase them out over time. The superintendent of schools would be responsible for assuring that the nonsystem schools or programs fulfilled the terms of their contracts. However, the superintendent and the district's administrative structure would play no part in the operation of these privately contracted schools.

Theodore Kolderie suggests a more encompassing transformation.[6] States, he suggests, could abolish school districts, eliminating the current monopoly on public education. The first step, he points out, is for a state to allow statewide choice, which is becoming less and less radical an idea. This overcomes the tyranny of residence determining where a student goes to school, and begins to change the mind-set that accepts that the buyer (student/family) is limited by what the local authorized seller has to offer. But, as many have observed, choice among schools in a district, and even more so among districts, will best serve those with the means to exercise their options to the fullest.

Attending school twenty miles from home is a much more real-istic proposition for a family with a parent or some other adult at home during the day who can provide transportation. Parents who work but want to be able to have some involvement in their children's schools and do not have transportation are not likely to send a child to a neighboring school district or a school on the other side of a city.

The second step in ending the monopoly is creating the oppor-tunity for more than one organization to offer public school "on the same piece of ground." Kolderie suggests a variety of public organizations a state might consider. A suburban school district could establish a school in a city; an urban school district could establish an alternative school for at-risk students in the juris-diction of a suburban community. Students would enroll in the district running a school but attend where they live.[7]

In addition to letting school districts operate schools outside their jurisdictions, states could recruit other public organiza-tions to establish and run public schools, or even entire districts. Among these are the colleges and universities in a state higher education system (many school districts already have arrange-ments approved by school boards whereby high school students take courses in institutions of higher education), local govern-ment sponsoring agencies, and the state itself. (North Carolina has created special schools drawing from the statewide popula-tion for the arts and math/science and Virginia for science and technology.)

The public organization sponsoring a school would not neces-sarily be responsible for running it. Organizations and agencies could contract with whatever group they chose that could pro-vide the educational program desired. This could be a corpora-tion, a group of educators, parents, or another public organiza-tion such as a college or university. Accountability occurs through the school's responsibility to its sponsoring organiza-tion, the contract to provide the educational program, and the influence exerted by families using such schools. Parents and students in a locality offering many choices could, indeed, vote with their feet but not have far to walk.

This model of public diversity suggested by Kolderie does not eliminate the traditional system but establishes real choices in a community, choices with which the school board would have to compete in quality if it decided to retain traditional public schools. As anyone who has had experience with attempting to establish alternative schools within the district establishment knows, unconventional solutions threaten what is already in place, and students are frequently actively discouraged from exercising such options. The exceptions are those few districts that have established magnet schools for purposes of desegregation wherein the selection of a school is made on the basis of the focus of the program and all students choose. However, the spectacle of parents lining up in the dark of the night to assure registration for their child in a certain school in Prince Georges County, Maryland, for example, has not resulted in wholesale change in other elementary schools to bring them into line with the most popular.

Removing School Boards as the Operating Authority for Schools

Many critics of the current system of school governance and operation concur that waiting for "market forces" to create change in the major cities will take too long. The system, they argue, has imploded in these districts. This has occurred for a variety of reasons, not all of which can be laid at the door of school boards. Boards, however, are not providing evidence that they can lead the city schools out of chaos. Beyond the paradigms of the connection between setting policy and running schools, there are other ways to think about configuring policy and operations.

ELIMINATION OF SCHOOL BOARDS

Ideas for structural changes in education governance suggested thus far preserve, even if radically altered, a local, separate governing or policy body for public education. The following options offered for discussion eliminate school boards. The first plan, while radical in that school boards are completely eliminated, requires the least change in the system and may very well occur in a major urban district in this decade. The second alternative essentially removes any educational policy role from local communities and is, therefore, an unlikely governance reform strategy. The third describes a possible new governance function responsible for all services to children and youth. The fourth option would be a radical policy change for states but would accommodate the value Americans place on local determination.

Governance of Education by Units of Local General Government

Mayor Flynn, as already noted, successfully asked the Massachusetts legislature to place the Boston public schools under the authority of the mayor and the city council through an appointed local school committee. Education policy for the city's schools is now naturally much more aligned with the political structure that makes policy for all other elements of city government.

Opponents cited all the arguments usually called forth in defense of the separation of education from general government—often perfectly legitimate in theory but clearly inadequate in light of the results from the present system of education governance in cities. The arguments center on the special focus on education that would be lost in a merger: critics envision political deals in which education needs are on the table along with potholes in the streets, the number of police on the beats, and garbage collection. There are still those who, with a straight face, say this change would make education "too political." Given the politicization of school boards and political pressures exerted by their constituents in many cities, this criticism hardly will carry the day for maintaining school boards.

As with any governance changes that may be discussed or tried, as in Chicago, there is no assurance of a dramatic improvement in the organization of educational services in schools or, more important, in the educational achievement of students. Unified governance could help to solve some problems in urban education, particularly in creating a more coherent system of support services linked to educational services. Accountability for public education would lie squarely with the mayor, rather than be diffused among a board of governors. The numerous sources of political pressures on a superintendent would be correspondingly reduced. In the present structure, enormous amounts of time and energy are expended by urban superintendents in responding to the political interests and pressures of individual school board members, taking away from the attention due the educational challenges of administering the school district.

Opponents of unifying governance have to recognize a major shift in the issues that have absorbed local government in recent years. Education is a major concern now because the economic and social viability of the cities is seriously threatened and education is viewed as key to their survival. Not all mayors or city councils are enthusiastic about taking on the problems of their cities' school systems, but there is not a mayor in office who would deny that education is a major issue.

A State System of Public Schools

In the heyday of state reform initiatives and major increases in state funding of public elementary and secondary education, there were both those who feared and those who cheered the prospect of a state takeover of the governance and operation of public education. Ideas surfaced for establishing regional governing districts that might be roughly contiguous with labor markets. This type of delivery structure might have regional boards appointed by governors or state boards, or governing boards elected by the region served. This would not necessarily have resulted in the elimination of separate governance structures for public education, but neither did it require their continuation. The proposal appealed to those looking for immediate and uniform implementation of state reforms and for strategies to eliminate the barriers posed by the need to gain the cooperation of hundreds of school districts in a state. However, there was never any serious attempt by a state to assume the operating responsibility for public education.

What appeared to be an unending escalation of direct state involvement in local education has been tempered, if not reversed, by the financial crises in many states. Not only have increases in state funding ceased generally, but states are reversing commitments to the existing levels of financial support. At the same time that states have been sliding financially, the driving intellectual and political forces in education reform have turned to the individual school as their main concern. The states will retain a vital role, but the focus will be less on prescriptiveness, fine-tuning, and mandating and much more on setting goals and objectives, defining expected educational outcomes, developing student assessment methods consistent with restructured curricula, and serving as a resource and support system. Taking into account this evolution in thinking, along with states' fiscal traumas, direct state governance and operation of schools is highly improbable. On the other hand, some serious thinkers are advancing ideas that would establish the state as the "licensor" for the delivery of local educational services, granting authority to individual schools and eliminating school districts.

Local Determination for the Structure of Governance

If continuing local control is an issue, states might allow localities to choose their form of public education governance. Lest one think this is a radical idea, cities over a certain population size in Ohio already may determine if they wish to have school boards. No city has exercised the option to reexamine its education governance, or even initiated a referendum on the matter. What does a state have to lose so long as its laws and regulations are observed? The local authority for operating schools might change, but accountability would be defined. And with local citizens making the political decision about governance, state legislators would avoid the political fallout that would inevitably accompany changing from one statewide system to another.

States might also exercise their authority to restructure governance in cities with populations of a certain size, or school enrollments over a certain number of students, but allow the majority of communities to continue or change their governance structure as they choose. Because the size of school district enrollment does not necessarily correspond to the degree of inherent problems—large suburban county districts such as Fairfax County, Virginia, and Montgomery County, Maryland, cannot be equated with Chicago and New York—the criteria for state-mandated reorganization of local governance might be based on the percentage of students who are economically disadvantaged, the average educational achievement of students, the ready availability of alternative public schooling suitable for a majority of students, or the depth of the need for a single, accountable local authority for coordination of education and other human services.

Any change that drastically alters the traditional governance structure will be fiercely attacked by powerful forces. One of the advantages of the radical route is that all the vested interests are equally threatened—school boards, teachers, administrators, even schools of education in the nation's colleges and universities. Any state that proposed mandating or enabling legislation to accomplish such reforms would get quick attention from all of the above. The pioneering state would send a very strong message that the condition of public education, specifically in the cities, cannot continue, and would stimulate public dialogue among all stakeholders in public education. That is what the nation needs.

Concluding Thoughts

A merica's "unique institution," the local lay board of education, has basically governed well as this nation grew from an agrarian base through rapid and awesome industrialization, while absorbing immigrants into society at a pace and magnitude unrivaled in modern times. School boards governed the one societal institution given primary responsibility for the assimilation of these waves of immigrants. Generations of laypersons presided over a system of public education that in time achieved the highest secondary school completion rate of any nation in the world and the highest participation in postsecondary education. The achievements of this largely voluntary system of local educational governance deserve respect.

We are now questioning the efficacy and attempting to reform the basic structure of schooling in this country. Governance cannot be excepted from searching analysis. The rapid urbanization and suburbanization of the nation's population, coupled with the changing demographics of youth, created unprecedented pressures on school districts and those who govern them. There is observable breakdown in the governance of the major urban school districts, wherein over 40 percent of our children are educated. We cannot ignore governance problems simply out of respect for the historical accomplishments of school boards. Nor should we, without thoughtful deliberation, decide school boards simply are not up to the task. Change for change's sake, a route Americans are all too inclined to pursue, would accomplish very little.

There are no easy answers to any of the questions we are asking ourselves about public education. Indeed, there may be as many answers as there are types of communities. Careful study of local governance may result in a reaffirmation of the current system with a commitment to strengthen and support local school boards, or it might determine, at least for some school districts, that radical restructuring of governance is required. We need intelligent dialogue to bring into sharper focus our expectations of how local school governance can lead the way to improved public schooling. Based upon the results of that dialogue, we can then begin discussion of informed recommendations about shoring up, reforming, or radically altering the current structure of local governance. A result of national dialogue might well be a recommendation to state policymakers to allow local communities to experiment with different governance models. But whatever the outcomes of a national dialogue, both the school board community and the national education reform agenda will be well served by thoughtful deliberations about our expectations and the condition of local governance of the nation's schools.

Notes

Introduction

1. John W. Gardner, *On Leadership* (New York: Free Press, 1990), pp. 15–16.

2. Ibid.; see pp. 11–22 for Gardner's discussion of the nine tasks of leadership.

3. Institute for Educational Leadership, *School Boards: Strengthening Grass Roots Leadership* (Washington, D.C.: IEL, 1986), preface.

Chapter 1

1. Institute for Educational Leadership, *School Boards: Strengthening Grass Roots Leadership* (Washington, D.C.: IEL, 1986).

2. "Critical Problems of Superintendents," Institute for Educational Leadership, Washington, D.C., 1991. "Critical Problems" is a transcript of oral interviews with superintendents of public schools.

3. IEL, *School Boards*.

4. David B. Tyack, *The One Best System: A History of American Urban Education* (Cambridge, Mass.: Harvard University Press, 1974).

5. John E. Chubb and Terry M. Moe, *Politics, Markets and America's Schools* (Washington, D.C.: The Brookings Institution, 1990).

6. Stephen K. Clements and Andrew C. Forsaith, eds., *Chicago School Reform: National Perspectives and Proceedings of a Conference,* The Educational Excellence Network and the Joyce Foundation, Chicago, 1990, p. 42.

7. William A. Firestone, Susan Fuhrman, and Michael W. Kirst, *The Progress of Reform: An Appraisal of State Education Initiatives* (New Brunswick, N.J.: Center for Policy Research in Education, 1989).

8. Michael W. Kirst, "Implications of Education Reform Trends for School Board Leadership," unpublished manuscript, 1990.

9. Chubb and Moe, *Politics, Markets and America's Schools.*

10. Jacqueline P. Danzberger, "A Study of School Board Effectiveness," unpublished manuscript, Institute for Educational Leadership, Washington, D.C., 1990.

11. The IEL school board self-assessment system incorporates a board effectiveness self-assessment, a report back to the board that provides mean ratings from individual members' assessment of their board, and an improvement planning process. The national demonstration of the system was conducted in the period 1988–90 with a 266 sample of boards across 18 states. This sample includes 70 urban school boards, 75 suburban boards, and 121 rural/small-town boards. In 128 of the school districts, superintendents also completed the assessment in order to give their perspectives on their boards' effectiveness to state school boards associations' facilitators working with the sample boards. It is important to be familiar with the self-assessment instrument in order to interpret findings from these national data discussed here and in chapter 3. The self-assessment instrument, the Inventory of Board Effectiveness, has fifteen sections corresponding to the fifteen Indicators of School Board Effectiveness developed from IEL's 1986 national study of school boards. Within each of the fifteen sections, members of a board individually and anonymously rate specific assessment items. There are from six to fourteen items per Indicator area. The Inventory uses a six-point rating scale that asks a board member to rate the degree of his or her agreement with the statement in terms of the board on which the respondent serves. Completed self-assessment instruments from all board members are scored, producing a mean rating for each assessment item, as well as a mean rating for each of the fifteen sections of the Inventory. The IEL analysis interprets a score of 4.0 and below as indicating a board does not perceive itself as very effective, a score of 4.1–5.0

as slightly to somewhat effective, and a score of 5.1–6.0 as generally effective. Interpretations of data such as these often tend to split statistical hairs or are treated as a report card, i.e., pass at this score, fail at that score. These data document the problem areas and areas of relative strength. The purpose of the Inventory is to help boards take a comprehensive look at their performance, define the areas in which they need to improve, and determine what they will do to improve.

The assessment items address a behavior, decision, action, or set of expectations that the board can control itself. In other words, the behaviors implicit in the assessment items are not dependent on outside resources or on the behavior of another government body or person. While the development of actual information systems for monitoring board policies would be the responsibility of the superintendent, the responsibility for assuring that such systems exist would fall to the board of education.

12. Jacqueline P. Danzberger and Michele Clark: *School Boards and School Restructuring* (Washington, D.C.: Institute for Educational Leadership, forthcoming); Paul T. Hill, Arthur E. Wise, and Leslie Shapiro, *Educational Progress: Cities Mobilize to Improve Their Schools* (Santa Monica, Calif.: RAND Corporation, 1989), p. 27.

CHAPTER 2

1. James W. Guthrie and Rodney J. Reed, *Educational Administration and Policy: Effective Leadership for American Education* (Englewood Cliffs, N.J.: Prentice Hall, 1986), p. 24.

2. Ronald F. Campbell et al., *The Organization and Control of American Schools*, 5th ed. (Columbus, Ohio: Charles E. Merrill, 1985), p. 53.

3. David B. Tyack, *The One Best System: A History of American Urban Education* (Cambridge, Mass.: Harvard University Press, 1974), p. 127.

4. Joel Spring, "The Structure of Power in an Urban School System: A Study of Cincinnati School Politics," *Curriculum Inquiry* 14 (1984): 419.

5. Tyack, *The One Best System*, p. 130.

6. Spring, "The Structure of Power in an Urban School System," p. 405.

7. Ibid., p. 410.

8. Institute for Educational Leadership, *School Boards:*

Strengthening Grass Roots Leadership (Washington, D.C.: IEL, 1986), executive summary.

9. Chester E. Finn, Jr., "Reinventing Local Control," *Education Week*, January 23, 1991.

10. Ibid.

11. John E. Chubb and Terry M. Moe, *Politics, Markets and America's Schools* (Washington, D.C.: The Brookings Institution, 1990).

12. Paul T. Hill, Arthur E. Wise, and Leslie Shapiro, *Educational Progress: Cities Mobilize to Improve Their Schools* (Santa Monica, Calif.: RAND Corporation, 1989), p. 27.

13. Ibid.

14. Michael W. Kirst, *Who Controls Our Schools?* (Stanford, Calif.: Stanford Alumni Association, 1984), p. 32.

15. Carol Smith Merz, "Conflict and Frustration for School Board Members," *Urban Education* 20 (January 1986): 401.

16. IEL, *School Boards*, pp. 7–9.

17. Kirst, *Who Controls Our Schools?*, p. 41.

18. Ronald F. Campbell et al., *The Organization and Control of American Schools*, p. 78.

19. Ibid., p. 80.

20. Ibid., p. 93.

21. IEL, *School Boards*, p. 14.

22. Robert Bendiner, *The Politics of Schools: A Crisis in Self-Government* (New York: New American Library, 1969), p. 21.

23. IEL, *School Boards*.

24. David Tyack and Thomas James, "State Government and American Public Education: Exploring the 'Primeval Forest'," *History of Education Quarterly* 26 (Spring 1986): 39.

25. Jennifer O'Day and Marshall S. Smith, "Systemic School Reform," in *The Politics of Curriculum and Testing*, ed. Susan Fuhrman and Betty Malen, forthcoming.

26. Harriet Tyson-Bernstein, *A Conspiracy of Good Intentions: America's Textbook Fiasco* (Washington, D.C.: Council for Basic Education, 1988), p. 110. This is citing data from the Association of American Publishers Industry Statistics, 1986.

27. Harriet Tyson-Bernstein, *Three Portraits: Textbook Adoption Policy Changes in North Carolina, Texas, and California* (Washington, D.C.: Institute for Education Leadership, 1990), p. 2.

28. Tyson-Bernstein, *A Conspiracy of Good Intentions*, p. 62.

29. O'Day and Smith, "Systemic School Reform."

30. Michael W. Kirst, "Who Should Control Our Schools?" paper

prepared for the Breckenridge Forum for the Enhancement of Teaching, Trinity University, San Antonio, August 18–21, 1987, p. 9.

31. Ibid., p. 13.

32. Jacqueline P. Danzberger, "School Boards: The Forgotten Players on the Education Team," *Phi Delta Kappan* 36 (September 1987): 53–59.

33. Ibid.

CHAPTER 3

1. Chester E. Finn, Jr., "Reinventing Local Control," *Education Week*, January 23, 1991.

2. John Carver, *Recommendations to the West Virginia Legislative Oversight Commission on Education Accountability* (Carmel, Ind.: Carver Governance Design, January 1991).

3. Jacqueline P. Danzberger, "A Study of School Board Effectiveness," unpublished manuscript, Institute for Educational Leadership, Washington, D.C., 1990.

4. David B. Tyack, *The One Best System: A History of American Urban Education* (Cambridge, Mass.: Harvard University Press, 1974), p. 76.

5. Ibid., p. 159.

6. Ann Bradley, "A Frustrated Boston City Council Votes to Abolish School Committee," *Education Week*, December 12, 1990.

7. Ann Bradley, "Rapid Turnover in Urban Superintendents Prompts Calls for Reforms in Governance," *Education Week*, January 30, 1991.

8. Margaret C. Hermann, "The Executive Lament: On Structuring CEO-Board Relations in the Public and Non-Profit Sectors," *Mershon Quarterly Report* (1987).

9. Oliver S. Brown, Robert S. Peterkin, and Leonard B. Finkelstein, "Urban 'CEOs': Untangling the Governance Knot," *Education Week*, March 13, 1991.

10. Ibid.

11. Bradley, "Rapid Turnover in Urban Superintendents."

12. Ibid.

13. Ibid.

14. Ibid.

15. "Critical Problems of Superintendents," Institute for Educational Leadership, Washington, D.C., 1991.

16. Ibid.

17. Bradley, "Rapid Turnover in Urban Superintendents."

18. Thomas A. Shannon, "Local Control and 'Organizacrats',"
Education Week, February 13, 1991.

19. T. E. Davidson, "School Boards and Superintendents: How
Are They Getting Along?" *Dialogue* 36 (May/June 1986): 5–7.

CHAPTER 4

1. Joel Spring, *The Structure of Power in an Urban School
System* (Toronto: Ontario Institute for Studies in Education/John
Wiley, 1984).

2. Institute for Educational Leadership, "National Support for
Collaboration: Needs at the State and Local Levels," report prepared for the Danforth Foundation, Washington, D.C., April
1991.

3. Jacqueline P. Danzberger, "A Study of School Board
Effectiveness," unpublished manuscript, Institute for Educational Leadership, Washington, D.C., 1990.

4. Julia E. Koppich and Charles T. Kerchner, "Educational
Policy Trust Agreements: Connecting Labor Relations and School
Reform," Policy Analysis for California Education, University of
California, Berkeley; Stanford University; University of Southern
California; Berkeley, 1990.

5. John E. Chubb and Terry M. Moe, *Politics, Markets and
America's Schools* (Washington, D.C.: The Brookings Institution,
1990).

6. Theodore Kolderie, "The States Will Have to Withdraw the
Exclusive," Public Services Redesign Project, Center for Policy
Studies, St. Paul, July 1990.

7. Ibid.

BIBLIOGRAPHY

Bendiner, Robert. *The Politics of Schools: A Crisis in Self-Government.* New York: New American Library, 1969.

Bowler, Mike. "Does Baltimore Really Need a School Board?" *Baltimore Evening Sun,* January 7, 1991.

Bradley, Ann. "A Frustrated Boston City Council Votes to Abolish School Committee." *Education Week,* December 12, 1990.

____. "Rapid Turnover in Urban Superintendents Prompts Calls for Reforms in Governance." *Education Week,* January 30, 1991.

Brockett, Diane. "Will School Reform Improve U.S. Competitiveness?" *School Board News,* February 18, 1991.

Brown, Oliver S., Robert S. Peterkin, and Leonard B. Finkelstein. "Urban 'CEO's': Untangling the Governance Knot." *Education Week,* March 13, 1991.

Campbell, Ronald F., Luvern L. Cunningham, Raphael L. Nystrand, and Michael D. Usdan. *The Organization and Control of American Schools,* 5th ed. Columbus, Ohio: Charles E. Merrill, 1985.

Carver, John. *Recommendations to the West Virginia Legislative Oversight Commission on Education Accountability.* Carmel, Ind.: Carver Governance Design, January 1991.

Cetron, Marvin, and Margaret Goyle. *Educational Renaissance.* New York: St. Martin's Press, 1991.

Chubb, John E., and Terry M. Moe. *Politics, Markets and America's Schools.* Washington, D.C.: The Brookings Institution, 1990.

Clements, Stephen K., and Andrew C. Forsaith, eds. *Chicago*

School Reform: National Perspectives and Proceedings of a Conference. The Educational Excellence Network and the Joyce Foundation, Chicago, 1990.

Committee for Economic Development. *The Unfinished Agenda: A New Vision for Child Development and Education.* New York: CED, 1991.

"Critical Problems of Superintendents." Washington, D.C., Institute for Educational Leadership, 1991.

Daley, Suzanne. "School Chiefs Dropping Out, Plagued by Urban Problems." *New York Times,* December 26, 1990.

Danzberger, Jacqueline P. "School Boards: The Forgotten Players on the Education Team. *Phi Delta Kappan* 36 (September 1987): 53–59.

———. "A Study of School Board Effectiveness." Unpublished manuscript, Institute for Educational Leadership, Washington, D.C., 1990.

Danzberger, Jacqueline P., and Michele Clark. *School Boards and School Restructuring.* Washington, D.C.: Institute for Educational Leadership, forthcoming.

Davidson, T. E. "School Boards and Superintendents: How Are They Getting Along?" *Dialogue* 36 (May/June 1986): 5–7.

Finn, Chester E., Jr. "Reinventing Local Control." *Education Week,* January 23, 1991.

Firestone, William A., Susan Fuhrman, and Michael W. Kirst. *The Progress of Reform: An Appraisal of State Education Initiatives.* New Brunswick, N.J.: Center for Policy Research in Education, 1989.

Gardner, John W. *On Leadership.* New York: Free Press, 1990.

Graham, Ellen. "In Inner-City Schools, Endless Transfers Hurt Some Students' Work." *Wall Street Journal,* November 14, 1990.

Green, Sarah. "Education Jumps to the Top of Voters' Worries List." *Wall Street Journal,* November 14, 1990.

Guthrie, James W., and Rodney J. Reed. *Educational Administration and Policy: Effective Leadership for American Education.* Englewood Cliffs, N.J.: Prentice Hall, 1986.

Hackett, Geraldine. "Learning Gets a Major Role in Classless Society." Reprinted in *Network News and Views* (Vanderbilt University), Nashville, January 1990, p. 106.

Hermann, Margaret C. "The Executive Lament: On Structuring CEO-Board Relations in the Public and Non-Profit Sectors." *Mershon Quarterly Report,* 1987.

Hill, Paul T., Arthur E. Wise, and Leslie Shapiro. *Educational Progress: Cities Mobilize to Improve Their Schools*. Santa Monica, Calif.: RAND Corporation, 1989.

Horsley, Lynn. "Feelings of Foes, Friends Run Deep." *Kansas City Star*, February 20, 1991.

Institute for Educational Leadership. *School Boards: Strengthening Grass Roots Leadership*. Washington, D.C.: IEL, 1986.

____. "National Support for Collaboration: Needs at the State and Local Levels." Report prepared for the Danforth Foundation, Washington, D.C., April 1991.

Kaplan, George. *Who Runs Our Schools?* Washington, D.C.: Institute for Educational Leadership, 1989.

Katz, Michael B. *Class, Bureaucracy and Schools*. New York: Praeger, 1975.

Kirst, Michael W. *Who Controls Our Schools?* Stanford, Calif.: Stanford Alumni Association, 1984.

____. "Who Should Control Our Schools?" Paper prepared for the Breckenridge Forum for the Enhancement of Teaching, Trinity University, San Antonio, August 18–21, 1987.

____. "Implications of Education Reform Trends for School Board Leadership." Unpublished manuscript, 1990.

Kolderie, Theodore. "The States Will Have to Withdraw the Exclusive." Public Services Redesign Project, Center for Policy Studies, St. Paul, July 1990.

Koppich, Julia E., and Charles T. Kerchner. "Educational Policy Trust Agreements: Connecting Labor Relations and School Reform." Policy Analysis for California Education, University of California, Berkeley; Stanford University; University of Southern California; Berkeley, 1990.

Leff, Lisa. "Desperately Seeking Superintendents." *Washington Post*, March 3, 1991.

Lutz, Frank W., and Lee-Yen Wang. "Predicting Public Dissatisfaction: A Study of School Board Member Defeat." *Educational Administration Quarterly* 23 (February 1987): 65–77.

Merz, Carol Smith. "Conflict and Frustration for School Board Members." *Urban Education* 20 (January 1986): 397–418.

National Civic Review 80 (Winter 1991): 2–64.

National Governors' Association. *Educating America: State Strategies for Achieving the National Education Goals*. Washington, D.C.: NGA, 1990.

O'Connor, Tim. "KC Hires New School Chief." *Kansas City Star,* February 20, 1991.

O'Day, Jennifer, and Marshall S. Smith. "Systemic School Reform." In *The Politics of Curriculum and Testing,* ed. Susan Fuhrman and Betty Malen, forthcoming.

Peirce, Neal R. "Boston School Board Demise Signals More Reform Turmoil." *Richmond Times-Dispatch,* December 30, 1990.

"Plan on Interagency Collaboration Approach." *School Board News,* March 6, 1991.

Reecer, Marcia. "Yes, Boards Are under Fire, But Reports of Your Death Are Greatly Exaggerated." *American School Board Journal,* 1989.

Rezendes, Michael, and Steven Marantz. "Council OKs End to School Board." Reprinted in *Network News and Views* (Vanderbilt University), Nashville, January 1991, p. 82.

Shannon, Thomas A. "Local Control and 'Organizacrats'." *Education Week,* February 13, 1991.

Spring, Joel. *The Structure of Power in an Urban School System.* Toronto: Ontario Institute for Studies in Education/John Wiley, 1984.

____. "The Structure of Power in an Urban School System: A Study of Cincinnati School Politics," *Curriculum Inquiry* 14 (1984): 19.

____. *Conflict of Interest: The Politics of American Education.* White Plains, N.Y.: Longman, 1986.

Tewel, Kenneth J. "Do State Takeovers Hasten Reform—Or Impede Progress?" *Executive Educator,* March 1991.

Tyack, David B. *The One Best System: A History of American Urban Education.* Cambridge, Mass.: Harvard University Press, 1974.

Tyack, David, and Thomas James. "State Government and American Public Education: Exploring the 'Primeval Forest'." *History of Education Quarterly* 26 (Spring 1986).

Tyson-Bernstein, Harriet. *A Conspiracy of Good Intentions: America's Textbook Fiasco.* Washington, D.C.: Council for Basic Education, 1988.

____. *Three Portraits: Textbook Adoption Policy Changes in North Carolina, Texas, and California.* Washington, D.C.: Institute for Educational Leadership, 1990.

Viteritti, Joseph P. "The Urban School District: Toward an Open System Approach to Leadership and Governance." *Urban Education* 27 (October 1986).

INDEX